GW01606256

DIVIDE AND RULE

DIVIDE AND RULE

Jan Mark

KESTREL BOOKS

For Tony Lacey

KESTREL BOOKS
Published by Penguin Books Ltd
Harmondsworth, Middlesex, England

First published 1979

ISBN 0 7226 5620 3

Set in Intertype Baskerville type by
Western Printing Services Ltd, Bristol
and Printed in Great Britain by
Billing & Sons Ltd
Guildford, London and Worcester

CONTENTS

The fool that will not when he may,
He shall not when he would.

PART ONE
Summer

I

THE river ran slowly there, embraced the city in a single, casual curve, and moved on, unimpressed. It was a wide, idle river, basking like a serpent under the high sun that laid brazen scales along its back, and drew loops of black shadow beneath the bridges. On the water nothing moved but the shifting light and a young man in a rowing boat, drifting downstream at ease, from bridge to bridge. Now and again he lowered an oar, left or right, to steady his course; turned his head a little to see himself safely under a span.

On his one side the banks were curtained by willow and chestnut that discreetly screened rich men's houses from the curious gaze of the common herd in the city across the water. Over there the trees had been felled and trimmed and now stood again with their feet in the river, supporting catwalks and landing stages. He steered into the middle of the stream to avoid these obstructions that reached out to delay him, as they did at other times. Today the boat was empty, his work was done, and he was going home; to the other bank.

Between Ram's Bridge and Priest's Bridge the great wall of the temple hung in a veil of shade above him. When the sun sank the veil was cast across the river like a net, but now, at late morning, midsummer, it hung straight and harmless. Nevertheless, he rowed more vigorously, to be away from it, resentful of anything that came between him and the light. Looking up, at the wall, he thought that it leaned a little, as he always did; each time a little more, and he bent his heavy shoulders over the oars until the boat slid under the centre span of the Priest's Bridge and the wall was hidden by nearer walls.

His father was in the temple at that moment, and his brother, and all but the most infirm of the servants. Perhaps all the city was inside the temple today, all but him. The river was deserted and the air silent except for the dip and slip of his oars in the stream. No matter how often men might turn their backs on the god throughout the year, at midsummer they went to the Festival and offered their homage as though they were bound by oath to do so, and they were not. They went with bad grace, for good luck. All but him. Then on the bank, beside a furtive bush that had escaped the massacre, he saw a bad girl playing truant from the Festival. She saw him too, and waved, and he waved. The world came to life again; he began to sing.

He had a terrible voice. When he sang aloud, dogs looked reproachfully over their shoulders and hurried away. The girl put her hands to her ears in exaggerated agony, so he stopped singing and laughed instead. As the river carried him by he heard her laughing too and he rowed on, smiling. His name was Hanno.

Beyond the Mill Bridge a white house stood by the river in a garden of lawns and terraces. Flowers trailed from leaden troughs and stone urns; here and there a statue looked blandly in at a window. Vines hung over the porches. Towards the river, however, the formal glory of lily and rose gave way to trees and fruit bushes and bean rows, enclosed by a fence of chestnut palings, and outside the fence grew the wilder grasses and the little flowers, long banished from the garden; sorrel and clover, daisy, mallow, loosestrife and spurge. Rude hemlock jostled against the palings and looked over the top; poppies stood up among thistles and died in a day; forget-me-nots lay in a blue haze with mint and cress among the rushes. An elder tree grew aslant the stream.

Hanno directed his boat towards the elder and moored it with a rope thrown round the trunk. He was inclined to stay there, lounging under the leaves and watching the flowers fall like stars into the water, but it occurred to him that his arrival might have been observed and he felt he owed it to his family to appear as though he had come home in desperate haste – but too late, alas, to accompany them to the temple. He scrambled up the bank, hurried across the warm grass and made a show of leaping eagerly over the fence, although he could step over it without any effort, being long in the leg, and sinewy.

As the younger son of the house he might have walked under the vine-draped porch and in at the front door, leaving the servants to mop up his muddy footprints, but as a working man himself, reluctant to make work for others, he went round to the backhouse and leaned over the half-door.

'Hulloa?'

His voice, when he didn't try to sing, was pleasant and penetrating. It rolled round the backhouse, into the kitchen, and the infirm servant came out to him; once his nurse, now an old woman, nurtured on country tales, who chose to believe that because he was the younger son he was necessarily an idiot too.

'You're late,' she said. 'It's almost noon.'

'I know I'm late,' said Hanno, patiently. 'I'm always late. When was I ever on time?'

'When you was young enough to be thrashed,' she said, looking as though she would set about him now, given half the chance.

'Yes, but no one ever did thrash me,' said Hanno. 'That's why I went to the bad. Is there anything to eat?'

'They waited and waited, till the last minute, but you never came.'

'Oh, what a shame,' Hanno said, gleefully. 'Oh, what a

pity. I shall miss the Festival. Oh dear. *Is* there anything to eat?'

'You have missed the Festival,' said Nurse, duty bound to sound severe. 'They'll be home again in an hour.'

'Eat,' said Hanno. 'Food.'

Hanno had gone to the bad in a boat. The boat had caused his father sorrow and shame in his old age and had given his brother Ivo an undeserved reputation for keeping low company. The knowledge that he himself was the low company saved Hanno from feeling too much remorse at the livelihood he had chosen. Two years ago, with his formal education complete and his tutor departed, he had been offered various inducements to take up an academic career. He knew people who had died of being cured. As it was, his separated Hanno from the last low ancestor who had eaten his bread in the sweat of his face. Hanno had declined all the inducements for equally various and well-published reasons, and for one which he kept to himself.

Ivo, who superintended the family business, offered to take him into the pottery, for ceramics was a gentleman's craft and would conveniently camouflage Hanno's predilection for mud and water. While his elders debated the matter Hanno completed a private deal and turned up one afternoon with the boat, whereupon he advertised himself as a waterman and earned a small but adequate income by ferrying travellers and freight up and down the river. Being honest and amenable he soon became well-liked and trusted – among his customers. At home, his father no longer argued that a gentleman should come and go by the front door, not the back, and Ivo's business associates were allowed to remain ignorant of the fact that the amiable lout loafing about in the kitchen yard was one of the family and not one of the servants. Old enemies smirked at the sight of gentry turned tradesman, and old friends sighed at the thought of such a good mind going to waste. Covertly or openly they commiserated with Ivo and his father. Relatives called him an ingrate or, worse, a throw-back. Hanno knew that he had hurt them badly, and if he in his turn were hurt he felt that he deserved it. But he kept the boat.

The boat was called *Anise*, and Hanno knew her namesake better than his father might have liked. He draped himself over the door, eating bread and cheese and thinking of Anise, lovely Anise, great big lovely Anise; not much above the eyebrows, but so much below...

'You might at least go and meet them,' said a complaining voice at his elbow.

'Dressed like this? I don't think they'd care for that,' he said.

'At least look as though you'd meant to go with them. You've plenty of time to change. Then you can run all the way and arrive out of breath. You don't fool me but you might fool them,' she said, gloomily. 'You won't get out of going tomorrow, I promise you.'

He said, 'I could be working tomorrow.'

'No.' Her voice turned unexpectedly firm. 'You can't miss the Choosing. You're of age, this year. They'll have your name down, somewhere.'

'I dare say,' said Hanno. 'But they won't choose me, so why go?'

'How do you know? It's the god that chooses.'

'Yes, well, he'll have more sense than to choose someone who doesn't believe in him, won't he? He's got his pride like the rest of us,' said Hanno.

'That's beside the point. You cause enough grief in this house. Turning up tomorrow won't be any skin off your nose.'

At the mention of his nose Hanno began to tug at it, unconsciously self-conscious. Someone had once remarked unkindly that he looked like a sheep, and he did. A handsome sheep, but a sheep for all that; one of the long-faced marsh breed that walked through mire, impervious to foot-rot. No one who had seen Hanno wading along the river margin, preceded by the questing prow of his nose, could fail to note the resemblance.

'Well, get on with it, then,' said Nurse, holding the door open for him.

'I didn't say I was going.'

'You're going.'

He conceded defeat and went in, through the kitchen, past the little garlanded altar that the servants had set up in humble emulation of the household shrine in the hall, to the alcove in the passage where a ladder went up to the attic. Nurse waddled behind him.

'Your trollop was here this morning. Can't you tell her to keep away?'

'Why?'

'Your father saw her. We said she'd come to help with the laundry. Some tale! That lass never did any work on her feet. She says to meet her tomorrow night, same place as usual.'

'Then I will. Don't call her my trollop,' said Hanno. Poor Anise. All flesh and no core.

'What is she then?'

He hated to tell lies. 'My doxy?' he suggested, with what he hoped was a disarming smile, and sprang for the ladder which he climbed to his room under the roof.

He slept there from choice, although not with Anise, since few people cared to hazard the ascent and follow him up. It was as he had left it, three days before, shuttered and cool. He dropped his gear on the bed, from which it slid to the floor where he let it lie, and went to open the low window in the gable. He threw back the shutters and immediately forgot what he was supposed to be doing. The window looked out over the garden to the river and he sat on the floor, his elbows on the sill, watching the water and drifting back the way he had come, upstream. He knew every tree along the bank, beginning with his own elder; then the limes, just now coming into flower, the willows, the chestnuts, the alders. He knew every crossing; first the Mill Bridge, then Priest's Bridge, Ram's Bridge, Cart Bridge, Horse Ferry; after the bridges the meadows, and then the villages; Goat Lees and Cow Lees, Alder Fen, Thorn Eye and Ram's Eye. In every village a tavern, in every tavern a girl. Every day another village, another tavern, another girl, more girls than he wanted. The breeze off the water lifted his long hair, and the river dissolved into a bright and marvellous mist in which the only thing he could see with any clarity was the end of his nose. By squinting ferociously he could have brought it all back again, but he had been rowing since sunrise, and the volatile river light had exhausted his eyes. He cradled his head in his arms and looked inwards, to the restful, shapeless shades that swam in the dark.

He had taken to the boat to save his sight. Much as he disliked to deceive, this was one secret he would never reveal to his family. Sitting with his tutor, day after day, surrounded by scrolls and books, he had discovered that each day seemed to bring his face closer to the manuscript, while other faces around him turned into approximate sketches. He could see his way about, clearly enough, but all the dear details of life began to escape him. He foresaw, with real terror, a day when the whole world melted before his eyes and he would be dependent thereafter on the eyes and hands of others; so when the tutor walked out of the house for the last time, he closed his books and began instantly to look round for a means of escape, and the river had offered him one. He missed reading more than he would admit, but since he had given it up his sight had become no worse and he reckoned that he was safe, for the time being at least. If anybody had once suspected his trouble he would have been seized and subjected to treatment; incantations, ointments, evil lotions, bandages round his eyes and hands to lead him where he did not want to go. He knew people who had died of being cured. As it was, his precaution of waving to anything that moved in case it recognized him was regarded as charmingly friendly, and his habit of poking his head forward as if peering over a high fence was thought to be simply one of his many eccentricities, along with his talent for tripping over and his manifest dislike of being handled.

In the meantime he had found out an interesting fact. Having grown up in the belief that women sought perfection in a man, he was amazed to discover that while he strode about unhampered, in daylight, girls would only smile shyly at him; but when dusk fell, and he blundered uncertainly into unseen obstacles, they fell on him, wormed his secret out of him and proceeded to act as though he were not merely near-sighted but sand-blind, gravel-blind, stone-blind even. They advised him to lie down in order, they said, to rest his eyes. It was his weakness they were after, not his strength. The exception, the sweet exception, was Anise. If he were generally faithful to Anise it was because she was too stupid to notice what was wrong with him. When he fell over the furniture she assumed that he had been drinking, which was all she had ever learned to expect from young men. They were therefore quite comfortable together.

'Are you going, or ain't you?' demanded Nurse, at the foot of the ladder.

'Come up and get me, why don't you?' said Hanno, drowsily, with good-natured malice. Of all the people in the house she was the least able to attempt it, if also the most willing.

'Have you yet changed your clothes? Because if you

haven't, there's no time. Get down here now and get out.'

'It won't take a moment.'

'Yes it will. I know you. You'll fall asleep on your feet while you're thinking about it.'

He had intended to change his coarse shirt and trousers for a tunic and hose, which was what everyone else would be wearing. 'I'm doing it now. Listen, I've got the chest open already, I'm looking...'

'Well, you won't find. I had the maid tidy that out while you was away. Rags, it was, most of it. Why you have to live like a rat in the roof I don't know. I'll keep your things down here in future, where I can see after them.'

Nagged beyond even his considerable endurance he went down the ladder, and foraged about the backhouse for something to wear, perversely turning his back on Nurse who squelched behind him, waving clean linen about his head like banners. His work clothes hidden under an old black caftan, he changed his shoes for sandals, jammed the gardener's wide-brimmed leather hat over his disordered hair and set off through the garden. Nurse leaned on the half-door and watched him go. The unfastened caftan flapped round his heels, snagging on rose thorns, and he lurched over the fence like a grounded fruit bat.

'Why not use the gate, for once?' she shouted after him, but he was too far away to understand. He turned, stuck a finger in his ear, shrugged madly and plunged into the long grass. She sometimes wondered if he might be deaf as well as half-witted, and having known him from infancy, often marvelled at his reputation for intelligence. Intelligence, in her opinion, was the brake that gave you pause to think before you spoke, and as Hanno normally said the first thing that came into his head she had no reason to suppose that intelligence was part of his equipment.

The gate, which he might have used for once, was not the imposing structure at the front of the house but a rickety wooden grid, held together with bindweed, at the vulgar end of the garden beyond the currant bushes, and the path that led from it to the Mill Bridge had been reclaimed by wilderness years before. Hanno was the only one who used it, and he stumbled through waist-high grass and burdock, to emerge on the steps by the mill befurred with pollen. Spearheaded seeds had tacked themselves into the caftan and a tendril of green briony was wound round his ankle like a pet snake. He fell up the steps on all fours, ran across the bridge and into the alley that led to the city.

Across the empty market place he ran, along Potter's Street where Ivo and his colleagues pursued their gentlemanly business, and thence through the lanes and hidden squares that lay between the commercial quarter and the temple. There were several good straight roads that would have taken him to it sooner, but he liked going round corners.

When at last he could avoid the temple no longer, he slowed to a sedate walk, his disgraceful hat set uneasily at a respectable angle and his thumbs hooked into convenient rents in the caftan. On reaching the lane that led up to the gate he removed the hat altogether, fastened a string or two, and sat down on a mounting block to pick the vegetation out of his skirts. He was fond of his father and very fond of his brother, and privately agreed that he caused enough grief in the house. He knew that his appearance would occasion even further distress.

A single chime of the temple bell spilled over the wall and rolled down the lane to the city, and at the same moment the two wings of the great gate swung inwards. The people came out.

They did not look like people who had, a few minutes before, stood in the presence of the god. They strolled and sauntered, chatted, squabbled, snapped at their wives, hectored their husbands and clipped their children round the ear. One courting couple, so closely wrapped that they seemed to be encinctured with a single, endless arm, stood on Hanno's feet and promised each other unimaginable joys until they realized that he was listening. Two men rolled by, locked in a savage fight while their women, ignoring each other superbly, sniped at the combatants with hairpins. Hanno recovered his feet, tucked them out of the way and sat back with folded arms to watch the mob go past; hundred upon hundred, thousand upon thousand; reflecting that if there were any honest men among them, he would not be sitting alone on the mounting block.

When the spate had dwindled to a trickle, he stood up and moved into the open gateway to look for his family. The temple courtyard was wide, and the steps that led up to the colonnade were at the far side, beyond the fountain. He cocked his head, covered one eye, slitted the other and finally made out the figures of his father and brother, in conversation with friends, standing in shade at the head of the steps. The temple faced east, but even in the morning, when the sun shone full through the colonnade, the interior was dim and the roof seemed to be supported on pillars of shadow. Hanno felt no desire at all to go any closer and was about to resume his seat on the block when he noticed that on the other side of the lane other people were waiting; a man and a woman and three little children. They stood together, close, eager and apprehensive, on tiptoe and peering anxiously towards the steps as if expecting someone to appear. Hanno, frankly curious and a little lonely, crossed the lane and said, 'Who are you waiting for?'

They turned to him, surprised: surprised that he should intrude, and then surprised that they were not offended by the intrusion.

'We are waiting for my son,' said the man among them, 'who was the Shepherd. Today he comes home to us.'

'He was a lovely Shepherd,' said the woman. 'Well, you've seen him. You'd know.'

'No,' said Hanno. 'I don't go to the temple. But I'm sure you're right.'

'There you are then,' said the woman, assuming that he had said what she expected him to say. 'He was a good boy, and they took him for a whole year. It's not right,' she went on, feeling obliged to register a complaint in spite of her pride. 'But you can't refuse, can you? It wouldn't be good luck. You can't say No.'

'Can't you?' said Hanno, who privately thought that someone should try saying no.

'He was a lovely Shepherd.'

'He did what he had to do,' said the father.

'A whole year!'

'The Shepherd serves for a year always. Always has. You'd think our lad was the only one, to hear her run on.'

'I cried all night when they chose him.'

'You went out and told all the neighbours.'

'And tomorrow, some other boy...'

'It's a soft option, if you ask me, cooling your heels in there for a year. All right for some...'

'He was serving the god...'

'He could have been earning his living. I had to pay someone to take his place in the market...'

'A whole year!'

Hanno stood before them and smiled. To address him they had turned their backs on the gateway, and could not see what he saw; a youth of about his own age, or a little older as he must be, crossing the courtyard with the faltering steps of one who had only just learned to walk. He was a country boy, with ingenuous eyes, dressed to his obvious discomfort in a white linen tunic with full sleeves, and white trousers, cross-gartered to the knee with fine leather thongs. Hanno sympathized with anyone who disliked new clothes and raised his hand to the boy before bending down to the agitated little mother and saying, 'I think your son is here.'

She turned, with the whole family behind her, and engulfed her lad single-handed. The father reached over her head and shook hands with him as best he could.

She cried, 'Those aren't the clothes you left in!'

'No, Mam; they give the Shepherd new clothes for the Festival.'

'But you ain't Shepherd any more.'

'They let me keep them,' he said.

'But where are yours? I spun the wool myself.'

'These are better, Mam.'

'How can you say that? My own hands. . .Is this how you come home? Finding fault with everything. . .'

Hanno felt that he had no place in this emotional moment and retired to his perch on the mounting block. After a while the family moved off, taking their lad with them. As they went by he turned back and looked, wistfully as it seemed to Hanno, towards the temple. There went one Ritual Shepherd who simply must have enjoyed his term of office. It was probably the only holiday he had ever had, or would have.

For that whole year, so grudgingly spared him, he had been of consequence, the ceremonial link between the god and the people. Clad in the ritual vestments he had stood, three times a day, as the living bond between heaven and earth, surety for the god's attention to his people. Tomorrow he would be back at his stall in the market and another Shepherd would be chosen in his place.

Hanno remembered that this year he was supposed to present himself as a candidate. If he did not, his family would be liable to a substantial fine, which they could easily afford although that would be poor consolation for having a son who would put the city's good luck at risk in order to suit himself. He would have to go. The Shepherd was chosen by divination, and he wondered from time to time how the process was rigged so that the right person was selected. Clearly it would not do if someone like himself turned up as Shepherd; there must be a loophole of some kind, through which the more unsuitable candidates could be dispatched. A matter of such importance surely could not be left to the caprices of an unseen god. Those who Dwelt in the Temple were professionals. They would know their business. He decided to pay careful attention to tomorrow's performance, since he couldn't get out of it, to see how it was done.

Across the courtyard two men were walking; another father and another son. Hanno stood up and went to meet them, bowing to his parent and wrapping an affectionate arm around his brother. Owing to the irregular hours of his work he had not seen Ivo for several weeks. Ivo returned the embrace, his father took his arm, and there was no word of reproach that he had failed to come back in time for the Festival. Ashamed of his habits they might be, but they loved him. He knew that should the impossible happen and *he* were chosen as Shepherd, a year later they would be waiting at the gate to welcome him home.

2

In the city the Festival was celebrated with riot and abandon in street and market place, and scandalous stories circulated for weeks afterwards. In common with others of their class, Hanno's family confined its rejoicing at Midsummer to a quiet dinner at home, inviting any relatives who happened to be unoccupied that evening. In Hanno's opinion, far too many relatives were unoccupied. Every year he intended to make his excuses and leave, to go out and investigate the riot and abandon for himself as soon as the meal was over, but every year, somehow, he failed to escape and sat dozing over the cheese and wine, eyes swollen with fatigue, while little known cousins and uncles talked of even lesser known cousins and uncles, and made acceptably sententious pronouncements on the season of the year. Tonight there were three heavy uncles disposed about the table, with aunts and progeny in full throat. The sunset bathed the company in a misleadingly rosy glow and lit on the glazed lip of a big-bellied pot in the centre of the board.

'A new vase?' said Ivo, and up-ended it between his spatulate thumbs. Being a potter himself he had a habit of turning everything upside-down to see who had made it. He examined the legend with an experienced eye, stood the vase on the table and rang it with his fingernail. It chimed. 'It's beautiful work.'

'It looks as if it might farrow at any moment,' said Hanno, who was sitting beside him. 'Lots of little vases, all over the table.' Ivo sighed and Hanno petted the vase contritely, to placate him. It seemed that his every comment so far had been punctuated by sighs from one side or the other.

'It's a gift from your great-aunt,' said his father.

'Isn't it the one we gave her last year?' said Hanno, blinking at it.

'I doubt that very much,' said his father, with considerable restraint.

'Will you be quiet,' Ivo muttered. 'She's here.'

'What?'

'She's here tonight. Three seats along, next to Uncle Olaf.'

'Oh.' Hanno stood up and looked down the table among distant and indistinct kindred. 'God's greeting Great Graunt – Aunt. A fruitful Midsummer to you.' He caught his foot under a trestle, put a hand on the table to steady himself and knocked a flagon to the floor. 'Aaaach, goddam it. . .'

'Oh, sit down; sit down,' said Ivo, tugging at his belt, and Hanno dropped back into his seat, waving affably at the outraged aunt. Across the table an ancient cousin who fancied herself as a diplomat remarked loudly, 'Has he not grown?' as though that were the one thing that could be honestly said in his favour. She beamed benignly at the brothers and addressed their father. 'Boys to be proud of: and so alike!'

'Like two fleas in one ear,' said Hanno. Ivo ripped a chunk from the nearest loaf and slammed it on to Hanno's plate.

'Eat that.'

'Why? I don't want it.'

'Eat it, I said.' Hanno gave him a puzzled look and sank his teeth into the bread. Seeing his brother safely silenced for the time being, Ivo turned his back and set about appeasing the rest of the party.

In fact they were not much alike. Where Hanno leaned forwards and peered, Ivo stood back and regarded. In the warm evening light he seemed to have come fresh from one of his own kilns, unevenly fired, black and terracotta by turns. Hanno, also dark, was not *so* dark, sallow rather than ruddy, and although younger was very much taller so that he looked like a second impression of Ivo in which the colours had been diluted in order to go further.

The meal had been a substantial one and the dry bread was going down with difficulty. In front of him was a flat wooden trencher bearing cheeses. The big mild ones were already laid waste by the depredations of the uncles, but round the edge, wrapped in vine leaves, were several small goat's-milk cheeses, their pungency sealed inside white scabrous rinds. Hanno took one and pinched it a little to see if it were ripe. It was. The rind split, the fluid interior shot out like a comet, rose in the air and made landfall in the lap of an adjacent uncle. Hanno, who was very tired and more than slightly drunk, put his head on the table and laughed until his face ached, and fell asleep while he was laughing.

He opened his eyes to candlelight. The party had broken up, the table was cleared, and on a nearby chair Ivo sat looking at him. Even in the subdued light Hanno could tell that Ivo's face wore that terribly familiar look of despair.

'Isn't it time you stopped playing with your food?' he said, wearily. Hanno recalled the sweet trajectory of the cheese and began to grin. 'It's not funny. Hanno, you're eighteen! Can't you sit at a table for two hours without insulting someone? Every time you open your mouth. . .'

'Ah, god, I'm sorry,' said Hanno. 'Really, I'm sorry. I didn't know the old – lady was here.'

'Exactly. You were too drunk to see who arrived.' Hanno let that pass, as he had to. 'But even if she hadn't been, there was no need to say what you did about the vase. That kind of thing gets repeated – like what you said to Cousin Walafrid.'

'I can't recollect saying anything to Cousin Walafrid.'

'I'm inclined to think that's just as well,' said Ivo, severely. 'Let's hope that no one else remembers, either.'

Hanno tried to check his widening smile and winced.

'I've split my lip.'

'You probably hit it on the edge of the table when you passed out,' said Ivo, intimating that this was no more than he deserved.

'I didn't pass out, I was asleep,' said Hanno, yawning self-righteously. 'I was up at dawn, remember.'

'You slept very soundly then,' said Ivo. He passed a hand over his face and smoothed away an incipient smile of his own. Hanno felt very sorry for him. Ivo had grown up assailed by cries of *Don't encourage the child*, and although Hanno could no longer be regarded as a child and stood a whole head taller, Ivo still suffered from the burden of his responsibility. 'It upsets Father,' he said.

'He shouldn't invite them here,' said Hanno. 'Down they come, every year, like buzzards. Is there any wine left?'

'There is, but you're not having it,' said Ivo. 'He wanted especially to have a talk with you tonight, but I persuaded him to go to bed instead. He has his health to consider.'

'I suppose that means I'll get it tomorrow.'

'It's already tomorrow,' said Ivo. 'You ought to be in bed yourself. You've a long day coming.'

'And you haven't?'

'I'm on holiday. You have to go to the Choosing.'

'Oh, I don't, do I?' said Hanno. 'Will anyone care if I don't go? They won't notice, will they?'

'Stop wheedling,' said Ivo. 'You are of age to be chosen, your name's on the list, and if the god wills it, you will be chosen.'

Hanno was always taken aback on being reminded that Ivo did believe, sincerely, in the god and in the attendant rituals. His father's faith struck him as eminently reasonable;

old men have strange fancies; but Ivo was only six years older than he was. He laughed. 'Think on it, Ivo. Can you see me in that sheepskin. . .with horns. . . ?'

'It was about that that Father wanted to speak,' said Ivo. 'On the whole, I think it's a good thing he didn't.'

'What was he going to say?'

'Advice on how to comport yourself if you were chosen.'

'Oh.' He didn't argue. 'You've been at a Choosing, haven't you? What happens?'

'I'm going to bed,' said Ivo. 'And I suggest you go too. You'll see soon enough what happens.'

'But how – ?'

'What?'

'How do they choose?'

'The god chooses,' said Ivo. 'He needs no help. He knows who will be his faithful servant for a year.'

'I'm glad to hear it,' said Hanno.

'There has never yet been a Shepherd in the family,' said his father, as they sat over a late breakfast. 'It would give me great pleasure if you were to be the first.'

Hanno kept quiet and fiddled with the wreath of ivy that Nurse had prepared for him, against his visit to the temple. Out in the country some of the old farmers still sacrificed a sheep at Midsummer, and the animal was led garlanded to the slaughter. He pulled the wreath down hard until it hung round his neck, and looked at his reflection in the silver bowl of roses on the window ledge.

'Baaaaa,' he said, softly.

Ivo's head swung round.

'Stop that.'

Hanno worked the wreath back over his ears and settled it so that it encircled his head, but horribly snarled up with his hair, which he wore hanging almost to his shoulders. He glanced once more at the rose bowl, to ascertain that he looked as stupid as he felt, and returned to his breakfast.

'I'll tidy you up afterwards,' Ivo hissed, leaning across the table.

Hanno glowered at him. When he was very small Ivo used to clean his teeth for him until the morning Hanno had bitten his finger to the bone. Ivo still fussed over him. They had lost their mother on the day that Hanno was born, already too large and untimely, and when he paused to think what Ivo had got in exchange he could have wept at the pity of it. He thought of it now and sat with bent head, unprotesting, while Ivo disentangled the ivy stems from his hair and removed sundry other foreign objects that were nestling in it.

His father, with unusual empathy, looked up and said, 'Your mother would have been so happy to see you now, my son.' Hanno, very moved by this rare lie, smiled back at him.

You cause enough grief in this house.

The Rite of the Choosing of the Shepherd began at noon. Ivo offered to walk to the temple with him and Hanno, feeling miserably conspicuous with his Festival clothes and foliate head, accepted gratefully. While his brother was dressing he went about the house and garden making various arrangements for his return. With a trip downstream to the harbour commissioned for next morning he stowed his gear in the boat, sent a verbal message to illiterate Anise confirming their meeting and went down to the end of the kitchen plot to inspect and reset his mole traps.

Ivo found him there, on hands and knees in the dirt.

'Why must you trap moles anyway?' Ivo demanded, dusting him officiously. He made further repairs to the ivy. 'This thing will look like a funeral wreath by the time you arrive.'

‘Should I care? A friend of mine at Thorn Eye promised to pay for as many as I could get.’

‘I can imagine,’ said Ivo. ‘What does he do with them?’

‘He’s the village healer. They’re a sovereign remedy for something, he says. Thank god I don’t suffer from anything that can be cured with moles,’ said Hanno. ‘You know – he boils them.’

‘It’s time we were going,’ said Ivo.

‘Go on, then. I’m almost done here. I’ll catch you up.’ Ivo hesitated. ‘What’s the matter?’

‘Do you think. . .perhaps you should go to the shrine first?’

‘No, I don’t,’ said Hanno.

‘It would please Father. He made an offering on your behalf, this morning.’

‘He knows I don’t believe. What good would pretending do?’

‘He still hopes. Would it hurt to keep him hopeful? He can’t understand how you could have lost your faith. No more can I. Now what are you doing?’

‘There’s another run here; two more traps. I would think more of your god,’ said Hanno, ‘if he did something. Miracles; strange things in the sky; earthquakes even. But he does nothing. He takes your offerings and gives nothing in return. He accepts worship, and says nothing. He demands a Shepherd – and what does the Shepherd get? Nothing. Except a year off work,’ he added, thinking of the last Shepherd. ‘I suppose that’s worth having.’

‘That’s not true,’ said Ivo. ‘He works in men’s minds.’

‘Maybe, but he leaves no evidence. See here, if you told me there was a great treasure in that molehill I’d be a fool not to look, wouldn’t I? But if I didn’t find it I’d know it wasn’t there. I wouldn’t call you a liar, but I’d say you were mistaken. You tell me there’s a god in the temple. I look. I don’t find him.’

‘Say that to yourself sometime, when you’re in a better temper, and you’ll see where the fault lies.’

‘I never lose my temper,’ said Hanno, equably. ‘You know that. Well, that’s it. All empty.’

‘A little anger might be good for you,’ said Ivo. With anyone but his brother he would have been on the verge of a quarrel. ‘Why should you always be happy, huh?’

‘I’m not, as it happens,’ said Hanno. ‘But on the other hand, why shouldn’t I be? I work at it.’

‘Time to go,’ said Ivo.

‘No moles today – hurray, hurray, hurray,’ Hanno sang as they walked to the front gate.

‘That’s not a very professional attitude,’ said Ivo.

‘I don’t really like killing them,’ Hanno confessed, apologetically.

‘Then why do it?’

‘I need the money.’

Ivo stopped with his hand on the gate, in the act of closing it behind them.

‘Hanno, you don’t.’ He was very shocked.

‘I do. Rowing a boat’s not the fastest way to the top of the tree.’

‘It wouldn’t be.’

‘You know what I mean.’

‘Only too well. You could have all the money you wanted – you’ve only to ask.’

‘From you and Father?’ Hanno looked him in the eye. ‘Do you really want to finance my affair with a stevedore’s daughter?’

‘*Hanno!*’

‘Yes. It sounds nasty coming from me, doesn’t it? But that’s just how you’d put it. Oh no. If I’m to live the way I want to live, I must pay for it.’

They were walking down the paved road towards the Mill Bridge. Ivo touched his arm.

'Do you have to live that way? Have you ever seriously thought about doing anything else? I'd help you all I could.'

They had this conversation fairly regularly and Hanno loathed it.

'I know you would, but it's not worth the effort. I couldn't be beholden to anyone; working at someone else's bidding, always shut in, always having to guard my tongue –'

'That wouldn't do you any harm.'

'I hate a closed door.'

Ivo stopped in his tracks but Hanno, not noticing, walked on.

'Wait!'

He turned and saw Ivo hurrying to catch up with him. He looked more than usually troubled.

'Hanno: had you considered. . . ?'

'What?'

'It could happen.'

'What could?'

'You could be chosen.'

'Ah, no. You can't believe that.' Hanno leaned against the parapet of the bridge and laughed. Ivo didn't laugh.

'I'll pray that you're not.'

'In spite of Father?'

'In spite of Father.'

'You really do mean it, don't you,' said Hanno, wonderingly. 'Come on, let's get this foolishness over.'

Some people, for good luck, poured wine into their wells, hung a ram's horn above the bed, buried iron beneath their doorsteps. For good luck, and without knowing why, they spat over their shoulders when the new moon rose, threw coins into the river at the time of spring tides, walled up a live toad in the foundations of a house. For good luck, and without knowing why, the city sent its sons to the temple, on the day after Midsummer, so that from among them the god might choose a Shepherd to serve him for a year. No one ever refused to go, or if he did, his family soon made sure that he changed his mind.

It was for good luck.

From all over the city the candidates converged upon the temple along the lanes and alleys and highways, under the flowering lime trees. As they all drew together in the lane that approached the gate Hanno looked them over, the pious and the profane, the most disparate among them alike in their formal dress, in their wreaths, in their age.

'I can't come any further,' said Ivo, halting in the gateway.

'But you'll wait,' said Hanno. 'Won't you wait?'

'Better not,' said Ivo, unhappily.

'Oh. Well. . .I'll see you when I get home,' said Hanno, suddenly uneasy at finding himself abandoned in this company.

'I hope so.' Ivo turned to go, then, to Hanno's considerable disquiet, he came back and put his arms awkwardly round his towering young brother. 'I hope so.' This time he went, without looking back.

Hanno entered the courtyard, shuddering. Even with the gates wide open he was uncomfortably aware of the oppressive wall that enclosed the place, forty feet high and continuous, with only that single exit, and that single exit almost always barred. On one side of the circling wall stood a second circle, the colonnade upholding the inverted saucer that was the roof; and inside that circle, a third; the sanctuary where very few might tread; only those that Dwelt in the Temple and one other: the Ritual Shepherd.

Hanno climbed the steps to the colonnade and wondered which of his companions would be inside the sacred circle tonight. It was at least two years since he had last been here, but as a child he had attended services regularly, and he recalled the strange little lean-to in the sanctuary, thrown up against the rail, that was the hut of the Ritual Shepherd; the place where he lived and slept, a divinely appointed interloper in the precinct, daily and nightly in the sight of the god.

The sanctuary was at the top of a further flight of steps. The well of the temple, between those steps and the colonnade, was the place where ordinary men might walk freely. Hanno, feeling very ordinary, walked about admiring the tiles on the floor. Each was moulded in relief to represent a flower and he moved from one to the next as though they were stepping-stones, rose, lily, mallow, clover, sorrel, aconite, spurge, but as more candidates came up the steps from the courtyard he turned shy and halted by a pillar, out of the way, where he might best see what was going on.

It seemed to be a boom year for prospective Shepherds. He had never imagined that the city held so many people of his own age. That was one of the drawbacks to being educated at home – so many friends and enemies never made. He looked enviously at old mates greeting each other. No one knew him. He did not love crowds or pine for company, but here he did not want to be alone.

Then he saw a face that he recognized. By each pillar in the colonnade stood a youth wearing splendidly elaborate, and elaborately useless, armour and carrying a long spear. They posed immobilized and rigid, as if it were they who supported the roof, and not the pillars. They were the Guardians of the Temple, holders of yet another ritual office, as opposed to the guards who wore rather more functional armour and stood at the gate; laymen, paid a wage for their services. Each Guardian faced outwards and the one by the next pillar to Hanno's was profiled sharply against the stone beside him. Hanno knew that snub nose and premature jowl from long ago. He had first seen them on a pugnacious little boy who had appeared in the meadow on the far side of the garden fence and, by means of well-aimed taunts and gibes, invited Hanno to come out and fight him. Hanno, tall even then, had hopped over the fence and laid him out in less than thirty seconds and after that they had knocked each other about fairly regularly, wisely concealing their bellicose friendship from their respective parents. It was, of course, Ivo who had discovered the source of Hanno's proliferating bruises and put a stop to their fun. Hanno often wondered what became of his sparring partner after that and now he knew: a temple Guardian, dedicated for life to the service of the god. Stranger things could happen, thought Hanno, without thinking very hard what they might be. He seemed to remember that the boy was called Dow, and hoped there would be an opportunity to speak to him on the way out.

High in the roof a bell rang once and the crowd fell silent. Across the sanctuary, from behind the altar, came an old man tented in embroidered robes that brushed his unshod feet, and followed by a boot-faced acolyte who walked with the assertive air of the born subordinate. The priest was empty-handed. The acolyte carried a plain wooden staff, tipped with the curling horn of a ram. When they reached the open gateway that broke the ring of the sanctuary rail they stopped and looked down at the candidates waiting below. The priest motioned the acolyte to step forward and took from him the staff. Without preliminary greeting he said:

'This is the Staff of the Shepherd, which is his to hold for the god in the year to come. One among you will have that Staff in his hand an hour from now. See to it.' The bell rang again. 'The Rite of the Choosing of the Shepherd has begun.'

The candidates looked at each other with uneasy smirks and solemn frowns. Among them came a youth wearing the armour of a temple Guardian, incongruously laden with a basket of dried beans. He returned their curious gaping with a self-conscious scowl and managed to look, Hanno thought, like a soldier caught looting by camp followers. They were about the same height and as the bean merchant passed Hanno he caught his eye, saw Hanno's involuntary smile, and moved on with an ugly grimace that made Hanno profoundly thankful that they were unlikely to meet again.

He mounted the steps and turned to face the candidates. 'Make a circle and sit,' he said shortly. Hanno found a place on the tiles and sat, between two others, cross-legged and alert. There was a certain amount of shuffling and muttering as the circle swelled and shrank, formed and re-formed. Hanno, who was sitting in a relatively stable section, glanced over his shoulder and noticed two things. The gates of the temple were closed and barred; and the Guardians, with their spears held out before them, were now facing inwards to the waiting circle in the well of the temple. There was no more smiling or quiet comment, no shuffling. The temple was silent. Hanno recalled that not long ago he had described the Rite of the Choosing as foolishness. He had laughed and Ivo had not laughed. Ivo had known what was coming.

The priest turned his back and walked to the altar. It was hidden from the candidates by the rise of the steps, but Hanno could see where it must be by the red-shaded lamp that hung above it, suspended on a brass chain. The priest raised his arms and demanded, in a voice that would brook no refusal, 'O god, guide the hand of your servant and be pleased to choose, through him, your Shepherd.'

The boot-faced acolyte took the basket of beans from the Guardian and advanced into the circle. He cleared his throat and looked all round him, as if expecting a threat to his person from behind.

'It is written,' he said, 'in the Book of the Ritual, that the god shall choose his Shepherd by the Rite of Three: by the Bean and by the Horn and by the Lamb.' He contrived to invest each workaday word with a sense of mystery, as if only thus could he bring himself to pronounce it. 'By these Three shall the Choice of the god be made known to us.'

'Why?' said Hanno. 'Why a bean?'

'Because the Book says so,' said the nearby Guardian, sharply, and clearly astounded that anyone should dare to ask.

'Does it say why?'

'Never question the Book,' said the Guardian. He leaned towards Hanno and added an informal threat of his own. 'If you open your mouth again you'll be sorry.'

Hanno subsided. Beans? Ivo maintained that parts of the Ritual were so old that they had existed before men could write, and were so obscure that even the Book, ancient though it was, could not explain them rationally. This was evidently one of the obscure parts. All right, then; bring on the oracular Bean.

'In this basket,' said the acolyte, 'there are as many Beans as there are of you. Some are white and some are red and you will each be given one. You will bow your heads and hold up your right hands and a Bean will be placed in each. Those who receive a white Bean will leave this place immediately, and the god will remember them kindly. Those who receive a red Bean will stay. On no account will you speak. On no account will you raise your heads or open your hands until you have been told which you have.'

Why? In case we try to change it? He did not care to risk asking out loud.

The acolyte began to pass round the circle, doling out beans like an almoner distributing relief rations during a famine. Hands were extended as he approached, some eagerly, some fearfully. Hanno was disappointed; it was all so easy, and all so obvious. A red bean for the good boys and a white bean for the bad ones; who could imagine that the god had a hand in it? If that were my god, thought Hanno, he would scatter the beans and fell that posturing fool with a thunderbolt and choose his Shepherd with a shaft of lightning, and then we should all know he had chosen. What pride can there be in being chosen like this?

An impatient foot tapped the tiles in front of him and he raised his hand, palm up, above his head. He felt something hard and cool pressed into it and his fingers curled in reflex.

Hanno was one of the last to be served and by the time the acolyte had stepped out of the circle the Guardian had stepped in. Moving from one candidate to the next he opened their hands. Some he dismissed with a jerk of his spear, and some he detained by laying the spear across their shoulders. It was as simple as that. Hanno, head bowed as instructed, felt him coming closer and gazed at the tiles in front of him. He wondered if Ivo's hand had ever touched any of these, clover, sorrel, woodbine, windflower. . .someone took his own hand and prised the fingers apart. Hanno looked up, startled, realized that it was his turn to be examined and waited for the gesture of dismissal. Instead, the spear came down sharply upon his shoulder and the Guardian moved on. Hanno lowered his hand and stared at it. He was holding a red bean.

The Guardian completed his circuit, waited to watch the last of the rejected hurry down the steps to the courtyard, and then said, 'Close the circle.'

Quietly, awe-stricken now, they slithered together. Hanno wanted to go up to the Guardian and say, Look, haven't you made a mistake? He wanted to get out now, as fast as possible; wanted to follow the last of the rejected down the steps, across the courtyard, out of the gate. He looked behind him and saw that the gate, which had opened for a moment to let them through, was closing once more. When he turned back, the acolyte was carrying a capstan into the centre of the circle.

A capstan?

Hanno, whose work took him often to the harbour, knew what a capstan was for. He had assisted in turning one on occasion, he and three others, straining every muscle. This thing in front of him was an effete apology for a capstan. It was made of bronze and stood about a foot high, squatting like a cat on daintily clawed toes. The Guardian came forward with the staff, thrust it through the hole in the head of the capstan and pushed it. It spun easily: no muscle required here. It reminded Hanno of a little device that was very popular in the gambling hall at the end of the Flax Market, and then he realized that this was exactly how they intended to use it.

'There are now sixty of you,' said the acolyte. 'And thirty times we shall spin the Staff. Those to whom the Horn is turned will arise and stand outside the circle. Begin,' he said to the Guardian.

The Guardian stooped to the capstan and the staff began its first revolution. Hanno watched it go round, with growing contempt. He had thought these people professional; a gaming table! Why not toss a coin? Why not throw dice? Why not throw loaded dice?

One after the other the candidates left the circle. When the curling horn came round to Hanno he scrambled up with nervous haste to join the second circle that was coming round the first; and when the staff had spun for the thirtieth time he turned quickly towards the colonnade and the gate, which was now open again. The Guardian addressed the candidates who were still seated on the floor.

'Return to your homes,' he said, 'and the god will remember you kindly.'

Those who were seated rose and scattered. Those who were standing looked at each other, wide-eyed, convinced that in some way they had been tricked; Hanno as convinced as anyone.

'Now comes the last of the Choosing,' said the acolyte. He pointed towards the gate in the sanctuary rail, where the priest was standing.

'We know that the god has Chosen already,' said the priest. 'Now he will reveal to those that serve him the Shepherd that he has Chosen.'

'Make another circle,' said the Guardian, 'and kneel.' It was a very small circle now. Hanno was beginning to feel angry; one senseless performance after another, and still no one had been chosen.

'What do we do now?' he muttered to the youth beside him. 'Draw for the shortest straw?' His neighbour inhaled with an offended snort and looked away, towards the gate of the sanctuary.

A man stood there, in the hat and cloak of a field worker; a real shepherd, carrying in his arms a little lamb. Hanno thought he recognized him since the river flowed by the pasture where the temple flock had its grazing, and he had stopped to chat, from time to time; but he was not certain, and this was no moment to introduce himself. The man's eyes were lowered piously as he came down the steps to the beckoning acolyte.

'This is the Lamb?'

'It is.' The acolyte whispered something to him. The man looked disconcerted and added, 'I do swear by the god that this is the Lamb.'

'Put it down,' the acolyte prompted him, irritably, and the lamb was set on its hooves, restrained by a plaited leash that the shepherd handed to the Guardian.

'The god has Chosen his Shepherd,' said the priest, 'and now the Lamb will find him.'

Hanno, increasingly perplexed, looked at the lamb. If this was the end of the Choosing, how was it done? So far as he knew, there was no way of bribing a sheep. He watched, very suspicious now, as the lamb was led into the circle and the leash released. The Guardian gave it a little pat on the rump and stood back.

The lamb bleated childishly and sidled among the flowers, spurge, aconite, lily, clover. Hanno was kneeling on roses and the thin cloth of his trousers was no protection against the glazed thorns. He fidgeted; the little hooves clicked. No one moved, but when he looked up through his eyelashes he saw that the priest was holding aloft a sand clock, and that the sand had only a little way to run.

How will it be done? They must have trained it to choose one from a circle, but which? Can sheep be trained? It's not that young, perhaps it has been doing this all its life. But how can it know. . . ?

The lamb went from one to another, its tail bobbing like a pliable truncheon. It paused by a candidate and for a moment all eyes were on him. Then it moved on, crossed the circle and back; and again; and back. It approached Hanno, skipped to one side, and retreated.

How does it know?

The lamb went once more round the circle and came back to Hanno.

No.

It stood before him on the tiles that Ivo might have made, rose, lily, hemlock, spurge. . .

No.

It stood.

No.

He was conscious of movement all round him, but still he knelt and the lamb stood and stood. Feet crossed the tiles, ran down the steps, through the courtyard; the gate opened and closed. He was almost sick with shock and stopped his mouth with the back of his hand, staring all the while at the little lamb, the instrument of his downfall.

The dice were not loaded after all.

3

He was pulled to his feet and propelled towards the steps of the sanctuary. The steps rose up like a wall, how would he climb them? and the lamb went ahead, skipping from flower to flower. Everywhere flowers, and feet; hands. At the top of the steps he was released.

'Take off your shoes.'

He crouched among the feet and unfastened his sandals. The battered wreath slipped from his hair and a hand plucked it away before it could fall to the ground. Another hand removed the sandals and more hands yet came down to help him up. He promised himself that in a moment he would regain control, shake off the hands and stand alone. For now, he must go where he was taken, and they took him towards the altar which was spread like a bed with sheepskins. The priest came forward to meet him, arms extended in gentle welcome. He too was without sandals; old men have strange feet.

'Oh, my son, my son,' said the priest. 'The god has brought you among us. You are standing in the sacred place.'

His mouth continued to open and shut. Hanno looked round at the sacred place, at the fleeces upon the altar, the ram's-horn candlesticks, the capering lamb.

'My son, what is your name?' The very air smelled of wool. 'What is your name? To the people you will be the Shepherd, but we must know who you are.'

The Guardian who had supervised the Choosing pushed his face between them.

'What's your name, Shepherd?'

His answer came out helplessly in a protracted bleat: 'Haaaanno.'

Perhaps his face compounded the felony. The priest reached him in three short strides, seized him by the shoulders and, with astonishing violence for one so frail, shook him back and forth until his flailing hair stung his eyes and the bones of his neck clicked in protest.

'Never. Never again. Never mock. Never, never, never. . .' The old man's fury escaped in outraged gusts. He let go suddenly, and Hanno went reeling back against the waiting wall of people.

'Never again,' said the priest, whose voice had lost all its unction, a wrung-out rag of a voice. He gestured to his attendants. 'We all know that the Shepherd must be unwilling, but –'

'But the Shepherd becomes willing,' interrupted the Guardian, glaring at Hanno with the same dislike that he had noticed earlier, and forgotten.

'Remember that the god has chosen you, my son,' said the priest. 'Your life is now in his hands.'

Hanno could have sworn that behind him someone whispered, 'And in ours.'

The priest held out the staff, with the coiled horn at the tip, and placed it in his hands. 'This is yours to hold for the god in the year to come. Ask the god that you may be worthy of it.' The staff, a crude stock of oak worn smooth by centuries of hands, slipped through his sweating fingers and he almost dropped it. A low murmur of disapproval curdled the air.

'Stand before the altar and ask the god that you may be worthy,' said the priest. He was pushed, not gently, shoved towards the high stone table where lay a hectic confusion of fleeces, horns, candles, vessels of clay, like the remains of a rudely disturbed dinner party. He remembered the aftermath of last night's party, and his own inept contribution to the celebrations; and Ivo's weary forbearance.

He found himself alone with his staff before the god. The others had retreated a little distance and he understood that they were waiting for him to pray.

There would be no forbearance here.

He prayed, after a fashion: 'Oh god, what will happen to me now?'

They left him alone, assuming that his stupor was indicative of deep devotion. With hunched shoulders and drooping head he looked as if he were praying and they withdrew, content. In fact he was cursing; a silent outfall of all the filthiest words he knew. He had no idea of what he might be cursing. He had only one thought in his head: he was in a mess and he had to get out of it. Waiting to come to the surface was the certainty that he was trapped, but unready to acknowledge this he drove it under with oath and blasphemy.

'Is that how you pray at home?' asked a voice behind him. He started, guiltily, afraid that they had sent a reader of minds to eavesdrop on him. 'Because if it is,' the voice went on, 'it won't do here. You must kneel.'

He looked round and there stood the pug-faced friend of his childhood, erect as an obelisk with ceremonial spear in hand, and regarding Hanno's slovenly slouch with extreme disfavour.

'Dow?'

'Hanno?'

He nodded and raised his head.

'I thought I recognized you as you came in,' said Dow. 'But of course, one cannot speak when on duty. The Rite of the Guardians prohibits it.'

Hanno blinked at the pompous formality of his tone. He had been a loud-mouthed little tough when Hanno knew him, with a stunted vocabulary and an animal repertoire of grunts. His voice had acquired a refinement that Hanno's had lost years ago. Hanno felt uncouth; a common enough experience for him, but one that rarely caused him as much discomfort as it did now.

'You've gone up in the world,' he said, bluntly.

'I was accepted into the Service of the Temple five years ago,' Dow said, reprovingly. 'My life is now an Act of Grace.'

And you've got a good opinion of yourself, thought Hanno, and for once had the presence of mind not to say it out loud. For all his new gentility, Dow still looked like a bruiser. He said, 'What am I supposed to do now?'

'Until you understand the Ways of the Temple, you will do as you are told,' said Dow. 'And I will tell you. I was Sent to Conduct you to your Hut.' Like the acolyte, he had the curious habit of solemnly stressing certain words, as though confirming them in the faith.

'I know where the hut is,' said Hanno. He could see it from where he stood, not twenty paces distant.

'I was Sent to Conduct you,' said Dow. 'Follow me.' Without the faintest hint of a smile he turned on the spot, shouldered his spear – almost taking Hanno's eye out in the process – and walked stiffly towards the ramshackle structure by the railing. Hanno followed, at a safe distance, remembering that Dow had always initiated a fight by trying to kick him in the groin.

The temple was built all of stone, even to the roof, a sullen mass of shade and substance. The iron rail round the sanctuary looked like a bracelet of man-traps, stood on end and linked with leg irons. The altar was a single slab of stone, balanced on others, but among all this weight and permanence stood the Hut, a little frame of hurdles with a tent-cloth stretched over them, just as any shepherd in a meadow might have. In the side of the hut that looked across the sanctuary to the colonnade there was a gap in the tent-cloth, made to serve as a doorway. Hanno observed at once that there was no means of closing it. Dow stood to one side and indicated that Hanno should enter. He stooped in at the doorway and remained stooping, for the roof was very low. On one side of the Hut, next to the railing, was an austere couch, with blankets, and beside the couch a roughly constructed table. There was nothing else. It was as bare as his attic room at home, but hostile; not his.

'You may sit on the Couch,' said Dow, ever so condescending.

'I'm damned if I'll sit on the floor,' said Hanno.

'If you are told to sit on the Floor, you'll sit on the Floor,' said Dow. Hanno propped his staff against a hurdle and sat on the couch. Dow also sat, on the other end of the couch. With two of them in it, the Hut was unbearably overcrowded. Hanno was accustomed to sleeping where he could when he was out with the boat, and some of the accommodation had been more cramped than this; but it had been his by choice; he could walk away. He noticed that from where he sat he could look across the courtyard, between two pillars of the colonnade, and see the barred gate, and the guards. He turned his head away and eyed Dow instead. Was it really Dow sitting here on the couch? Was it really Hanno sitting here on the couch; Hanno who had a boat to row, and a girl to meet, and mole-traps to inspect, a brother who hoped to see him tonight? It finally dawned on him that none of these commitments would be fulfilled. The only reality now was Dow, and the Hut, and the barred gate: the Shepherd.

He said furiously, 'I can't stay here. *I can't stay here.*'

'You must,' said Dow, in a voice as tight as stitching.

'No.' He didn't move from the couch but he fancied that he was running towards the gate, his hair streaming behind him. The gate fell flat beneath his feet and he was out.

'You have been Chosen. You are the Shepherd.'

'You don't understand. I have to go.'

'I do understand,' said Dow, suddenly and unexpectedly sympathetic. 'Remember, I've seen five Shepherds before you. The Shepherd is always unwilling, at first. The Book says so. But you will soon be one of Us. I do understand – and so must you. There is no way out after the Choosing.'

'I thought – anyone but me.' He was terribly ashamed to be saying this to Dow, of all people, but unable to stop himself he stammered, 'How could they choose me when there were so many others? It *must* have been a mistake.'

'The god Chose you. He knew who he wanted,' said Dow.

'How can I be Shepherd?'

'They all say that. Do you think you are Unworthy?' said Dow, solicitously. 'We are all Unworthy. But Trust in the god. At least you can put your Trust in the god. Think how much worse it would be for an unbeliever.'

But I am an unbeliever.

He didn't say it. Just in time, he didn't say it.

'You may rest,' said Dow. 'And I will call you when the Priest wishes to see you. You will have no duties today: your Life begins tomorrow.'

It ended an hour ago, you fool.

He said, 'When can I see my family?'

'Of course you can see your family,' said Dow.

'When?'

'Are you worried that they may be wondering what has happened to you? Don't worry. As soon as the Choosing was finished, a messenger was sent with the Good News. Your family will be rejoicing for you at this moment.'

'They can save their rejoicing till next year,' said Hanno, biliously.

'You could always write to them.'

'I want to see them.'

'Write a little Note. Someone will deliver it.'

'I have a boat on the river. What will happen to it? I had to collect cargo in the morning. I have to meet someone tonight.'

'That will all be taken care of.'

'Moles...'

'What?'

'Moles,' Hanno said, drearily. Lucky moles. Perhaps the moles had gathered together underground, swaying in earthy ecstasy as they prayed to their blind velvet god to deliver them. 'Save us,' they said. 'Let him suffer as he makes us suffer.' 'All right, boys,' said the mole god. 'We'll put *him* in a trap for a bit and see how he likes it.' 'Oh, thank you god,' said the moles, and sacrificed their finest worms as a token of their appreciation.

When he raised his head, Dow had left him and he was alone in the Hut. He looked again towards the gate. In the courtyard it was still a summer's day. In the city it was still a summer's day; outside the wall the river still ran, as it would be running in a year's time on another summer's day.

I want that year. It's mine. I want it.

What right do they have to take a year from me? Let them find some other who doesn't need it. How can *I* be Shepherd? I must tell them, I don't believe. Tell them, I'm sorry, your god has made a mistake this time. He must choose again.

If you knew what I thought of your god you would cast me out in shame that you had ever let me set foot inside his sanctuary.

He noticed that from time to time people approached the gate, paused to speak with the guards and were let out through a small wicket.

It's worth trying.

He left the Hut and walked quickly across the tiles of the sanctuary, rose, mallow, lily, hemlock, with a fresh surge of anger as he noticed that he was barefoot, and remembered that his sandals had been taken from him. The gate in the railing at the head of the steps was closed. Was that supposed to deter him? He stepped over it, as he stepped over the fence at home, and went down the steps, across the tiles of the well, rose, lily, woodbine, spurge, windflower. The Guardians were back at their posts by the pillars in the colonnade and he descended the steps to the courtyard backwards, watching them, daring them to break their rule and challenge him. Still in reverse he walked across the courtyard until his ill-used feet told him that the dilapidated pavement was no place to be without shoes. Even then he continued to cast a surly eye behind him, every few seconds. None of the Guardians moved, or even looked at him.

He passed the fountain where a girl sat, launching flowers on the water and sinking them with pebbles. It was surely a sign of his preoccupation that he didn't notice it was a girl until he was well past her, but by this time he was almost at the gate. Unlike the Guardians, the guards reacted as soon as they saw which way he was headed. Hanno stood looking from one to the other.

'May I go out?'

'Who are you?' said the left-hand guard.

'He's the Shepherd, that's who he is,' said the other. 'Ain't you the Shepherd?' he said, turning to Hanno.

'Yes.'

'Then you don't go out. Get your hand off of that wicket, it's locked. Go back to your Hut, Shepherd.'

Hanno retreated to the fountain where the girl with the flowers sat and watched him. Dazzled by the bright strands of water, he could not make out her expression, but he recognized a note of amusement in her voice and knew that she was smiling.

'God's greeting, Shepherd.'

He responded to the sound of a smile which he could not see.

'My name's Hanno,' he said, moving round the fountain to reach her. 'What's yours?'

'I am Nola. You are the Shepherd.'

'May I call you Nola? Won't you call me Hanno?'

'You may call me Nola. You are the Shepherd. Go back to your Hut, Shepherd.'

He was in no mood for taking orders. He walked round the perimeter of the courtyard, at the foot of the wall. The wall was sheer and smooth, without a foothold. He watched a beetle coming down and a spider going up. It was a big fleet-footed spider with hairy legs, and he stood with his head tipped back, following its wiry ascent of the white cliff, until it was lost among the flies in his eyes. He supposed that it reached the top and went down the other side but he could not see it and he could not follow.

He came to a smaller wall, set at an angle to the greater, with an archway in it, and in the archway a wrought-iron gate. On the other side of the gate he saw a garden, with flowers and lawns, vines, bushes and bean rows; a static statue and a living man with a hoe. The man with the hoe saw him and came up to the gate.

Hanno said, 'May I come in?'

The man with the hoe shook his head.

'Go back to your Hut, Shepherd.'

He went back to the Hut and sat on the couch, watching the hump-backed shadow of the temple extinguish the light in the courtyard. He looked at the wall and feared that in winter the sun would never rise above it. The temple had its own seasons, its own dawn and dusk and long midnight. Under other circumstances he might have admitted that the air was warm and that the birds in the courtyard sang as loudly as the birds by the river, but he sat cold and deaf with his chin on his fist, gnawing his lip. It was early evening, but already the temple was dark. The sanctuary candles were unlit and the only living light was the red-shaded lamp, a sole, miraculous star above the altar, seemingly afloat and becalmed in the gloom. Hanno went to the doorway of the Hut and stood there, staring at it. In his hazy eyes the sharp spark diffused to a deliquescent sphere and everything else was invisible. He was as blind as a mole in this light, but he knew where he stood. He stood on roses.

Almost imperceptibly the lamp moved, swinging on its unseen chain as if a draught had disturbed it. Hanno looked quickly to the altar. Expecting to see nothing, he saw nothing. The shadows were so thick an army might have gathered unnoticed there; but there was nothing wrong with his hearing. Something had moved and stirred the air that set the pendant lamp in motion. Something had spoken.

'*Shepherd.*'

'The Priest will See you now,' said Dow, coming quietly from the other direction. Hanno looked at Dow and back to the altar. Nothing.

The priest sat in his apartments, in a wide white room that overlooked the walled garden where the sun still shone. Hanno was brought before him and abandoned in the middle of the room where he stood alone while the old man gazed vacantly at the ceiling. Hanno imagined charitably that he was occupied with matters of the spirit, and whiled away the minutes by watching two girls in the garden who sat on the turf and plaited flowers into their hair.

It is not all darkness.

'My son,' said the priest, and Hanno's head came round reluctantly. 'My son, are you rested?'

How did one address a priest? Sir? My lord? Your reverence?

'Yes,' said Hanno.

'Are you ready to be told of the Rite?'

Hanno did not answer. Was this the moment when he should explain that he would never be ready?

'It is a simple Rite, as it needs to be, for the Shepherd is unwilling. The Shepherd is always unwilling.'

That was the second time he had been told, or the third. Who cared, anyway?

'I think, my son, that you are more unwilling than most.'

If only you knew how unwilling!

He said, 'I shouldn't be here.'

'The god Chose you. It is his Will that you are here. Let me explain to you why you were Chosen.'

Hanno looked up expectantly, imagining that some astonishing error would be revealed, but the priest was thinking in more general terms.

'Those of us who Dwell in the Temple are here by our choice. We entered the Service of the god because it seemed to us right. We were Called, but had we wished to do so we might have disregarded that Call. But the Shepherd cannot choose. He is Chosen. He has no Will. He is unwilling.'

'Why?' said Hanno. 'I have a will.'

'Hanno has a will,' said the priest. 'The Shepherd has no Will. It has always been so. The Book demands it.' He smiled at Hanno. 'But he becomes willing. In the end, and when he goes, he goes consenting.'

'Does the Book demand that as well?' Hanno could not suppose that anyone would fail to leave this place consenting. 'How do I – does he – become willing?'

'Never question the Book,' said the priest. 'The Shepherd needs to know nothing. It is enough that he is here.'

Tell him; tell him now that you do not believe. He will understand.

Yes, but what will he understand?

He said, 'I can't be your Shepherd.'

The priest said, 'My son, you *are* the Shepherd. The

Choosing is done. There can be no change now. Even were you a sworn unbeliever, there could be no change now.' His withered face swelled with kindness. He would understand nothing.

'Tell me about the Rite,' said Hanno.

'It is a Rite of Standing,' said the priest. 'The Shepherd stands before the people and he stands before the god. He is the medium through which prayer is heard and answered. He calls upon the god in the name of the people and upon the people in the name of the god. He is there to be seen.'

'But why do you need me to call on the god? Wouldn't he listen to you, sooner? He knows you.'

'Yes, but the people know you. Whoever the Shepherd may be, the people know he is one of them.'

'Not many people know me,' said Hanno.

'They expect to see a Shepherd and they see a Shepherd. Who he is does not matter.'

'Then why me?' Hanno cried, in a last effort to steer the dialogue his way.

'All that is spoken of,' said the priest, with finality. 'All that is done. Tomorrow you will stand before the people for the first time. Dow will tell you what to do, and really, you will find that it is very little, after all. You will find that it is a very easy life – when you become willing. Now you may go. Prepare yourself.'

'How?'

'You will be told how.'

'One thing more –'

'Go back to your Hut, Shepherd.'

The priest turned his eyes back to the ceiling. Hanno waited, to see if there might be any more information forthcoming, and then found his way to the door. Out in the garden the long shadow of the wall had reached the near edge of the lawn, but the girls still sat there, their hands full of flowers.

The priest's room opened into a corridor and on its left was another door which must surely lead to the garden. Hanno had his fingers round the handle before a voice detained him.

'Shepherd.'

Holding a torch and standing at the other end of the corridor was the Guardian who had supervised the Choosing.

'Where are you going?'

'Into the garden, I hope,' said Hanno, and turned the hoop of the handle. The door began to open but before he could set his foot over the sill Dow came out of the darkness on his other side. The Guardian with the torch came down the corridor and they outflanked him.

'No,' said Dow. 'Not yet. There are other things to see first.'

Hanno thought of disregarding them, if only to see what would happen – and because he wanted to be in the garden air, free from the smoky confines of the passage – but the Guardian carried his torch like a fiery sword, and Dow's voice held no invitation to argument.

'This is Egil,' said Dow, introducing the Guardian and managing to imply that Egil and Hanno were likely to become great friends. Hanno doubted it.

He found himself walking between them, back to the temple. The priest's apartments were reached through a doorway at the side of the sanctuary and in this wall were other doors, some open, some barred. Here cressets burned in iron brackets, and Egil extinguished his flame.

'Where do all those doors lead?' said Hanno. 'Or is that something else that the Shepherd need not know?' Egil appreciated the irony in his voice and blocked his path.

'One thing the Shepherd should know: he is the Ritual Shepherd, not the Ritual Fool. I'll leave him with you, Dow,' he said, as if another minute in Hanno's company was more than he could endure. He opened a nearby door and disappeared behind it.

'This is the Hall of the Guardians,' said Dow. 'And that door there, leads to the Hall of the Handmaidens. In here, the Hall of the Mechanicals –'

'The whats?'

'Mechanicals. The masons, gardeners, launderers, dairymen, cooks. You may never pass through any of these doors. This is the cookhouse, where you may go, but I won't take you in there now. They'll be preparing the evening meal, and you won't be able to eat it.'

'I would,' said Hanno.

'I mean, you will not be allowed to eat. Or sleep,' he added casually. 'Tonight you must Fast and Pray.'

'How often must I fast and pray?'

'One hopes that the Shepherd will Pray continually,' said Dow. 'But you won't have to Fast again until you leave us, unless you Transgress in the meantime. But you won't be leaving us for a long time,' he added, encouragingly. 'Although then, I'm afraid, you have to Fast for a week.'

Hanno did not pursue this depressing information. He had enough to occupy him right now. 'What's in here?' he said, tapping the next door.

'The Robing Room,' said Dow. 'You'll see in there tomorrow. This is the Bath House.' He opened the last door of all. The bath house was reached through a dark slype that smelled of moss and cold stone. Dow opened a second door at the far end and they stood in a roofless enclosure of marble columns, with a cistern sunk into the floor. 'The Shepherd must come here at least once every day.'

'What for?'

'To Purify himself.'

'You mean I should wash?'

'Bathe.'

'Why me in particular?' said Hanno. 'I bathe every day anyway,' he added, beginning to be offended.

'Not just you,' said Dow. 'We all come here, who Dwell in the Temple. You, me, Egil. . .The women have their own pool.'

They returned to the sanctuary. 'Now listen carefully,' said Dow, 'because I shan't see you again until the morning and you will not be able to speak to anyone after your Vigil begins. You will remain in your Hut until you hear the Bell strike once. Then you will take your Staff and go before the Altar and there you will Kneel until dawn. Pray.'

'What shall I say?'

'Pray from the Heart,' said Dow, paternally. Hanno thought, Good god, he's younger than I am. He's not natural. Someone should pickle him. 'There are no Words prescribed for a Vigil. The Prayers should be all your own. Now, may the god look kindly on you. Do you want to ask me anything before I leave?'

'Where's the privy?' said Hanno.

4

IT seemed that the Guardians worked in shifts. Beneath the summer sky that would never grow entirely dark, those who had stood in the colonnade since early evening left their places and returned to the greater darkness of the temple. Simultaneously another platoon stomped through the doorway beyond the sanctuary, with martial stride and much clanking, and went out to guard the temple against the forces of the night. Torches flared briefly and threw up attenuated shadows from floor to roof. Voices echoed among the columns and Hanno distinguished Egil's ill-natured tones above the rest. The signal for the change-over was the single stroke of the bell, and he was so intent on determining whether Egil was coming or going – and if coming, exactly where – that it was a while before he recalled that it was supposed to be a signal for him too.

He took the staff and wandered, dazed, into the darkness, finding his way to the altar by watching the sanctuary lamp, and holding the staff before him as a probe. When it struck stone he halted, stood the staff upright and climbed down it, hand over hand, until he was kneeling. Some sharp excrescence jabbed him in the knee. He was kneeling on roses again. He put his hand to the floor in search of a smoother flower. The tiles were large and square and the decoration was worked in accurate detail; here spurge, here mallow, lily, aconite. Smoothest of all was clover, so he knelt on clover, clasped wood, smelled sheepskin and tried to think himself into a green meadow, among flowers and trees and living sheep. It was not difficult, for he was only half convinced that he was in the temple anyway. It was impossible that he was in the temple, and in it moreover for a whole year, while the world, unthinkably, went on without him.

Ivo, you didn't pray hard enough, or else no one was listening.

He looked up at the altar.

Oy, you: why didn't you listen to my brother? Without thinking he spoke aloud and cut himself short. The Shepherd calls upon the god in the name of the people. *Oy, you.* He began to laugh, soundlessly; hopelessly.

In the sanctuary night was everywhere. Surely only a cat could see him now? He was not used to kneeling for any length of time; even the clover made an unsympathetic hassock and the thought of sneaking back to the Hut was very appealing. So long as he returned to the altar by dawn, no one would ever know he had been away, and he was about to put the thought into practice when he heard, on the other side of the altar, a small sound, like mice, followed by a restive rustling; rats? Hanno was indifferent to rats and rats were indifferent to ritual; they might be company for each other. He had heard of prisoners in deep dungeons who tamed rats and kept them for company and he toyed with the idea of taming a rat of his own, which he envisaged perched on his shoulder with long pink fingers reverently folded while he stood before the people: the Ritual Shepherd's Ritual Rat. He crouched on all fours with the staff ready beneath his hand, acknowledging regretfully that old habits die hard. Should the Ritual Rat now appear, his first instinct would be to whop it with the Ritual Staff; a very appropriate quietus. *Splat.*

There was no further sound so he began to back away, in the direction of the Hut, standing upright as he went, but before he was halfway home he heard the sound again, no hypothetical rat or mouse this time, but the formed and finite sound of a human footstep; not boot or sandal but the damp slapping of naked feet on tiles and coming towards him. Reluctant to run up against some prowling acolyte in the dark he hastened back towards the sanctuary lamp and ran up against the altar instead. The footsteps stopped and the rustling began again, accompanied by the unexpected sound of munching. A man *and* a rat? A man eating a rat? A rat eating a man? Hanno clung to the edge of the altar and peered over the top of it, trying vainly to see what lay on the other side.

He whispered, 'Who's there?' No one answered him but a faint soughing of breath confirmed his suspicion that his company was close at hand. Someone had been posted on the other side of the altar to make sure that he stayed where he was put. His first reaction was to go back to the Hut anyway, assuming that he could find it, and leave the stertorous sentry to follow if he could. Happily imagining him floundering about for the rest of the night he took a step backwards, noting inconsequentially that he stood one foot on clover, the other on roses, when he heard the footsteps behind him. If only a cat could see him, this fellow had the eyes of a cat. Swearing softly he knelt down again, holding the staff across his thighs and prepared to use it as a trip-wire should the opportunity present itself. He was too angry to fall asleep now.

Dawn was a long time coming. The temple became truly silent until it seemed to Hanno that even swallowing his own spit produced an echo like a stone dropped into a well. He kept his position as best he could, but every time he moved to ease his weight something else moved too. At last the sky began to bleach, like a row of towels strung out between the pillars of the colonnade. Hanno saw his hands grow pale round the black staff and decided that, whatever anyone else might think, this was dawn indeed. He sprang up, with a defiant crack at each knee, and collapsed against the altar. His feet had gone to sleep and he hung on to the staff, effectively hobbled, waiting for them to wake up. Round the corner of the altar came something that was not a rat, being the same height as a man and moving on two legs. It stopped, crouched, looked up, and tiny red lights pricked the darkness as the sanctuary lamp was reflected in unseen eyes. A ragged whisper came out of it:

'Shepherd.'

Hanno discovered that his feet were awake after all and began to retreat. He was not superstitious, but this thing that had come up out of the floor was uncongenial company in the half-light. It lurched after him.

'Shepherd.'

He crashed into the sanctuary rail and rebounded, to his way of thinking in quite the wrong direction. A ratty hand wrapped itself round his wrist and its owner drew him close.

'Shepherd?' It was still too dark to see it clearly, but the thing stank reassuringly of unwashed humanity rather than of the grave.

He said, 'What do you want?'

The thing nudged him confidingly, as if about to tell him a dirty joke, and said, 'The world is in a wheel, and the world turneth, and the wheel turns not.' It had the most commonplace voice with which to relay its revelation; gossipy, almost.

Behind them a door opened, and brisk footsteps crossed the tiles. The thing remarked, 'Behold, the Guardian comes, all dressed in gold, with the stars of heaven about his head.'

Dow, wearing a white caftan and with a towel hung round his neck, leaned over the railing, and Hanno's murky friend disappeared as suddenly as he had come.

'Good day, Shepherd,' said Dow. 'May the god remember you kindly. I see you've met Aram.'

*

Hanno was Conducted to the bath house, along the dank passage of the slype.

'Did he frighten you?' said Dow.

'Who – Aram? No; but he gave me a start.'

'It must have been a shock, coming across him in the dark.' Dow was off-duty and so was his voice. 'We should have warned you,' he said, opening the door at the far end of the slype.

'I didn't mind him in the dark. It was seeing him that was the shock,' said Hanno, beginning to think that the creature had been planted there to test his nerves.

'It must have been.' Dow flung the caftan from him and made an extravagant plunge into the cistern, where he swum up and down with powerful strokes. Three strokes took him from one end to the other. Hanno undressed and followed him more slowly. He was accustomed to running water, either a pump or the river; the stone cistern reminded him of a fish tank, where captive carp waited for meals, not their own.

'Who is he?'

'Who is who?'

'The man with the message.'

'We'd all like to know that,' said Dow. 'He's mad – you probably guessed? But quite harmless.'

'The Ritual Maniac?'

'He has no part in the Ritual,' Dow snapped. 'He comes and goes as he pleases. But the god looks kindly on lunatics. Mind you, he thinks he is part of the Ritual.'

'Isn't it time someone told him he's mistaken?' Hanno contemplated a year in Aram's noisome aura.

'He wouldn't understand; and it's bad luck to cross a madman, everyone knows. The Book says, The god is tenderest to those whose wits he has taken.'

'It could be wrong.'

'That's sacrilege!' said Dow, shockingly affronted.

'Never question the Book.' He dived, taking his indignation with him, and Hanno thought he was cooling off until a hand gripped his ankle and pulled him under, holding him there until he comprehended the error of his ways. By the time he had fought back to the surface Dow was out of the water, towelling himself dry with horrible heartiness for the time of day. He looked calmly on Hanno's efforts to recover his breath and his composure, and said,

'Guard your tongue, Shepherd. As to Aram, ignore him if you like, but don't laugh at him. It's safer not to laugh at anyone,' he added. He put on the tunic that he wore under his armour and opened the door to the slype.

'Where are you going?'

'I'm on duty at sunrise.' He scooped up a bundle of linen and began to leave.

'Those are my clothes you've got there,' said Hanno.

'We that Dwell in the Temple put on clean Raiment every day,' said Dow, managing to convey, once again, that Hanno's personal habits fell short of civilized expectations. 'So must you – in future. You'll get used to it.'

'But that's all I've got. Come back, will you,' Hanno yelled after him, starting to climb out of the tank. Dow looked round the door.

'You'll find the rest of your garments in that cupboard,' he said. 'Get dressed and go into breakfast.' The door closed behind him.

Hanno hauled himself out of the water and looked in the cupboard, expecting to find something conspicuous that it would be his ill-fortune to wear in public from now on, but the clothes were his own, packed in the canvas bag that he took with him in the boat when he went on long journeys. When not in use it was kept under his bed in the attic. How did it come to be here? Angry and suspicious and half-drowned he pulled on the first things that came to hand and ran after Dow.

Meals were taken in a long hall adjoining the cookhouse. The eaters sat on long wooden benches at long wooden tables with candlesticks aligned down the middle. From the doorway Hanno saw a dwindling perspective of planks and thought they were sitting in a tunnel. The draught that blew in with him sent the candle flames streaming into the tunnel and black smoke shimmied upwards. The light was poor, but sufficient to show him every head turned in his direction.

'It's the Shepherd,' said one voice, replete with boredom.

'I don't care who it is,' said another. 'Tell him to shut the door.'

Observing that they were as much unimpressed by his status as he was, Hanno fancied himself among like minds, if not friends.

'I was looking for Dow.'

'Tell him to shut the door.'

'If you want me to shut the door, tell me so yourself,' said Hanno, who had been about to shut it. Instead he held it open and looked round for the speaker. Immediately a figure rose at the other end of the room and stalked towards him between the benches. As it came close it resolved itself into a squat youth with eyebrows that met in the middle, giving him a permanent scowl. He stared at Hanno, turned deliberately and addressed the ubiquitous Egil who was sitting near the top of the table.

'Tell him to close the door.'

Hanno looked down at his stocky antagonist. He could have buttered the wall with him, only he had no wish to start a fight on his first morning. He had no wish to start a fight at all. In growing bewilderment he said,

'Either tell me yourself or shut it yourself.'

Egil stood up. 'Shut the door, Haaaanno.'

This echo of his unfortunate introduction produced an uproarious reaction. They found it immoderately funny, and the unanimous laughter sent the candle flames flaring in all directions. Hanno saw how one humiliation took root in another and closed the door.

'Now sit down.'

He sat.

'You're in for a distressing year, Shepherd, if you mean to go on as you've begun,' said Egil, resuming his place.

'Where's Dow?' said Hanno. There was a wooden trencher in front of him and it began to fill with water as his hair dripped into it.

'Dow is on duty. Do you think it is pleasing to the god to appear like this among his servants? Your nose is running.'

'Who brought my clothes from home?'

'You might at least dry your hair.'

Hanno wiped his head with his arm, cursorily, like a cat. 'Who did?'

'A man.'

'What kind of a man?'

'Why, one like us, with arms and legs,' said Egil, reasonably. 'A messenger went to tell your family that you had been Chosen and this fellow came back with him. He brought other things, but of course we could only allow him to leave the clothes.'

'One of the servants?'

'He said he was your brother,' said Egil, elaborately uninterested.

Hanno leaned across the table. 'My brother came here? Ivo? Didn't he ask to see me?'

'He asked,' said Egil.

'And wasn't allowed?'

'You were occupied,' Egil said. 'Praying – or sulking.' Hanno looked at him sharply, but Egil's face was smooth with indifference. 'We couldn't disturb a Shepherd at his prayers. Look, are you going to eat anything?'

'No. Damn it, no.'

‘Water is coming out of your ears,’ said Egil, as if he had been dowsing for it. ‘What were you doing in the bath house? We only expect you to bathe.’

‘Ask Dow,’ said Hanno.

‘When I ask you a question, answer it,’ said Egil. ‘When I give you an order, obey it. In an hour you will stand before the god, and you will appear worthy of your office. Go back to your Hut, Shepherd,’ he said, his tone suggesting that he knew very well how the command was beginning to rankle, and Hanno went back to his Hut, experiencing the novel sensation of embarrassment.

Adversity had never troubled him. It made him laugh, or sometimes it made him swear and he laughed afterwards. At the moment it looked as if he might never laugh again. He seemed to hear his predecessor’s mother in her clamorous indignation: A whole year!

What shall I do? said Hanno, gazing at the flowers on the floor until they faded away, rose, aconite, mallow, spurge. Ivo, what shall I do? He was not only trapped but lost, with no notion of his next move, because he had no notion of his next thought. It was time to begin laughing and he could not. He saw nothing at all laughable in his situation and sustained anger was making his head ache. This too was something new. He felt ill, and he was never ill. He lay back on the couch, his fingers braided into the fringes of the blanket, and began to understand slowly just what he might do to himself; or rather, what the Ritual Shepherd might do to Hanno. He had never before been so angry for so long, and yet the last Shepherd had come out of the temple with tranquil eyes, unscarred by self-inflicted wounds.

What shall I do?

His eyes closed and disquieting pictures began to form. If he went on as he was, it could be only a little while before someone guessed the truth, and even that would be no help.

'Even were you a sworn unbeliever,' the priest had said, 'there could be no change now.' There would be no change, but they would hate him. Egil disliked him already, had turned his very name into an insult. If the rest, and there were so many of them, followed Egil's example, Egil's prognosis of a distressing year could turn out to be a massive understatement. If, like Dow, they believed that their lives in the service of the temple were acts of grace, they would see his presence among them as an act of desecration.

More fools they, he said, for accepting a ritual that lands them with someone like me.

But they believe that their god chooses the right man. How if I showed them they were mistaken? They wouldn't hate the god, but they would hate me.

It was a painful thought. He liked to be liked and he was used to it.

Surely they want to like their Shepherd, and already I've upset them. If I stay...

No, there's no question about that. I can't get out of it. I *shall* stay, and I shall keep them happy; for all our sakes. But chiefly for mine.

He opened his eyes and saw the drab tent-cloth sagging in a depressed bulge, a few feet above him.

I'll have that down, for a start. It's like living under some great bum.

A Guardian, barefoot in the sanctuary, looked in at the door and saw him lying there.

'Are you unwell?'

'Thinking.'

'Soon One will come to Conduct you to the Robing Room. Be ready, Shepherd.'

'I am ready.'

'I mean, be on your knees. Be found at Prayer.'

The one who came to conduct him to the Robing Room

was Egil. It appeared that he and Dow were never on duty at the same time.

Never alone. Hanno wrenched his face into a smile.

'Are we going to the Robing Room?'

'Why are you so eager, all of a sudden?' said Egil.

'Once I've put on the Vestments, it will all seem so much Easier.' It's not so difficult to talk like them, he thought. Can I keep it up?

'It's not meant to be easy,' said Egil. 'You aren't on holiday.'

'Easier to Understand.' This is the one I have to watch. I don't trust him and he doesn't trust me. 'Shall we go?'

'Not that way,' said Egil, as he prepared to step over the railing. 'I don't know what you did for a living before you came here, but I can see there was no discipline in it.'

'No. No, there wasn't,' said Hanno, thinking of the simple river, and following Egil to the gate of the sanctuary.

'Dow says you come of a good family. No one would guess.'

'When can I see my family?' Egil paused in the gateway and put on the soft shoes that he had left there. 'And when can I have my sandals back?'

'When you need them.'

'Who says I don't need them now?' Hanno muttered. 'Supposing I want to go out.'

'Out of the Gate? You won't need them for that,' said Egil. 'Once the Shepherd is in the Temple he stays in the Temple. He might be allowed to visit his home, later on,' he said. 'When he becomes willing. Much later on, in your case, I would think.'

'Oh, I shall become willing,' Hanno whispered. 'You can't imagine how willing.'

Egil opened the door to the Robing Room. It was a dim interior, darkly curtained and carpeted, with dull lamps and a false ceiling of smoke that floated level with the lintel of the door. Yesterday's acolyte coughed in a corner.

'The Shepherd,' said Egil, and left him there. The acolyte was either deaf or unmannerly. He made no sign that he knew Hanno was in the room, and stood with his back to him, engaged in sewing a patch on a torn caftan which he held close to one of the little lamps. Hanno lounged among the curtains for a while, watching this unlikely seamstress and wondering what the women were for if the men did the sewing. He had seen three of them yesterday. Surely he hadn't imagined them?

Yesterday.

A sand clock decanted itself in the corner. Yesterday morning he had eaten his last meal. This morning he had breakfasted on spleen. His empty stomach chimed protestingly against his spine and the acolyte condescended to look round, as though summoned by bells.

'That's an unseemly sound, Shepherd,' he said.

'You try standing around with a gut full of wind,' Hanno retorted.

'And that was an unseemly remark. Why is the Shepherd here?'

'I've come to get dressed,' said Hanno. 'Why do you think I'm here? For the fine fresh air?'

'I was speaking the Rite of the Robing,' said the acolyte. 'You should reply, The Shepherd comes before the Master of the Robes to be clothed in the Vestments.'

'How could I know that?'

'You are here to learn. Now, say it.'

'The Shepherd comes before the Master of the Robes to be clothed in the Vestments,' said Hanno. It was his first official statement and he felt that it should have a more appreciative listener to receive it.

'Stand forth, Shepherd,' said the acolyte. 'Well, you're a wreck, I must say,' he complained, forgetting the ritual in his dismay. 'How did you dress this morning? With your eyes shut?'

Hanno made a noncommittal noise that could be taken for an apology by anybody who chose to think it was one. The acolyte turned himself on a snarl and opened a locked cupboard behind the curtains. Hanno looked over his shoulder. In the bad light the cabinet seemed to be inhabited. A bulky torso lurked in the shadows, headless, with the head on a shelf beside it. Hanno considered and rejected half a dozen unpleasant comments and stood back as the acolyte reached into the cabinet and lifted out a pair of athletic imitation shoulders from which hung the Shepherd's Ritual Sheepskin. It was a jerkin, made of two whole fleeces that were joined at the shoulder. Hanno recalled having seen the thing displayed on previous Shepherds and took comfort from the thought that although curious it was not ridiculous; on winter days ordinary shepherds might indeed protect themselves against the weather with such a garment. Today, however, was likely to be hot.

The acolyte raised the sheepskin and began to pray over it, requesting that the god should make sure that this year's Shepherd wore it with honour and brought no shame upon it. Then he reached up and lowered it over Hanno's head. The fleece was thick and pressed warmly against his neck, clasping him tighter than a brother. It smelled overpoweringly of old sheep, old Shepherds, old smoke, old incense. He thought wildly, I'm too young for this.

The acolyte advanced on him, swinging a length of chain.

'What's that for?' Hanno said, alarmed.

'The Shepherd is not required to know,' said the acolyte, and for a moment Hanno thought the chain must serve some dreadful purpose which would become apparent only when he was wearing it. It was made up of bronze links, each as thick as a finger. It clanked ominously as it came nearer. It was a belt, and with a second prayer concerning the worth of the belt and the worthlessness of the wearer, the acolyte wound it twice round Hanno's waist and fastened it with a hinged link. It was a tight fit and sank into the fleece. Hanno felt its weight and contracted from it, even while the greater weight of his suspicion was lifted from him.

The acolyte returned to the cabinet and brought out the head, a disagreeably realistic clay cranium that served as the Shepherd's deputy when he was not wearing the head-dress himself.

The head-dress was of unyielding leather and it closed over Hanno's thick hair like a second scalp, covering his ears and cutting off the sound of the acolyte's prayer on its behalf. On either side a great curling horn came down and forward, blinkering his eyes, so that he could no longer see sideways without turning his head. What he could see was powerfully concentrated between the horns and he thought, A cure? then dismissed the idea as the acolyte brought his mealy face close to the narrow aperture and mouthed at him.

'Go now to the Altar.'

'What?'

'Go now to the Altar. The Priest awaits you.'

'Yes. . .thank you. . .' He began to leave.

'You should now say –'

'What?'

The acolyte put his finger under the left horn, lifted it slightly and bawled, 'Stop shouting!'

'What should I say?'

'Get out,' said the acolyte, and watched him forage among the curtains in search of the door.

After the suffocating vapours of the Robing Room, the cool depths of the temple washed over him like water, but the sun was rising, and by the time he had walked round to the altar he was sweating in the grip of the head-dress and the odorous embrace of the sheepskin. Looking back he saw, to his disgust, that he had left a trail of moist footprints across the tiles. The priest was waiting for him at the altar.

'The Shepherd comes into the Holy Place.'

The gate was open.

'Rejoice with us on this your Day of Dedication.'

The gate was open and people were walking under the arch and into the courtyard. Of the torrent of worshippers that had flooded the temple at the time of the Festival, this was all that remained, a few faithful droplets.

'Approach with Reverence.'

If it's open now, to let them in, it must be opened again afterwards, to let them out. Sooner or later. . .

'Shepherd!'

I could get out if I tried. If things get too bad, I will try. . .

'What are you looking at?'

'Uh?'

He had been standing with his head turned right round, his face hidden from the priest by the helix of the horn, staring towards the gate. He had seen nothing and, therefore, heard nothing.

The gate was closing.

'Come, Shepherd,' said the priest, turning stern. 'The god sees you. Approach the Altar.'

The gate was shut.

'Take the roof off?' said Dow. 'Are you mad?'

Hanno turned on him a beseeching look that was only partly assumed.

'I have a boat.'

'What's that got to do with wrecking the Hut?'

'I work in that boat – worked – I almost lived in it. I was always out of doors. I used to sleep in the open.' If I couldn't avoid it. 'Dow, you'll have to be Patient. I was never one for regular worship; I expect you realized that?'

'I was beginning to,' said Dow, looking very earnest. Oh, he's loving this, thought Hanno. What he'd really enjoy is to have me grovelling on the floor while I told All.

'But out in the fields, I felt very close to the god. I felt that I understood. . .things,' he went on, lamely. 'I'm so *confused*, here. And so shut in.'

'I'm glad you told me this,' said Dow, as though Hanno had said something worth hearing. 'Every one wants to help you, and you haven't made it very easy for us.'

'I know,' said Hanno, abjectly, looking at the floor.

'We'll do everything we can to make you happy in your Service.'

'I know.'

'But why do you want to take the roof off the Hut?'

Grief, I might as well talk to the wall, Hanno thought. He hasn't understood a single word.

'I-feel-shut-in,' he articulated slowly, wrapping his mouth round every word. 'I-can't-bear-to-be-shut-in, I-shall-go-crazy.'

'The god will help you,' Dow murmured, soothingly. 'The god will not let his servant suffer.'

'I think the god would not mind,' said Hanno, cunningly, 'if I slept beneath his roof instead of my roof.'

'The god would be offended if you spurned his hospitality.'

'Hospitality? Spurned?'

'It says in the Book, that the god caused the first Shepherd to live in a Hut, and you know what. . .'

'Yes,' Hanno said, hurriedly. 'I interfere with the roof and you drown me?'

Dow's understanding smile unravelled. 'Once you would have been tied to a pillar and flogged for your levity.'

'I would?'

'That pillar, there,' said Dow, to impress upon him that these times were not too far distant.

Hanno looked at the pillar in question, since it was clearly expected of him. He had had his ears boxed from time to time, but he had never been beaten. He couldn't imagine that anyone would want to beat him. Dow saw that sweet reason had the whip hand and softened.

'You must ask for guidance.' He dropped a reassuring paw on Hanno's arm. 'You won't be left to struggle alone. I should think about your Deficiencies,' he advised, kindly. 'That might help. Just wait for the Noon Service, and think about your Defects.' Hanno's eyes widened at the prospect.

He can't have got like this by himself. Someone must have taken his mind out and put a wind chime in its place. He doesn't talk, he just makes noises.

'Remember, you're not alone,' said Dow. 'After all, we're still friends, aren't we?'

Yes; but I liked you better when you tried to send my front teeth out at the back of my neck.

'Yes, Dow.'

5

He had feared unnameable things; dark practices, suffering, endless indignities, and, after all, he was only bored. After seven days he was so bored he could scarcely keep his eyes open. True, being told continually what to do was an indignity of a sort to one accustomed to doing exactly as he pleased, but having nothing to do was infinitely worse.

He had absolutely nothing to do; no work and no recreation. His only exercise was anger, and he had always prided himself on his even temper, so he clung to it, stubbornly, refusing to lose it.

During the services all those who Dwelt in the Temple turned out in force and heavily outnumbered the few worshippers who straggled in from the city. When Hanno went afterwards to the Robing Room, to remove the vestments, they were still there, forgathering in groups, but when he came out again only minutes later, the temple was deserted. Where did they go? What did they do?

'What shall *I* do?' he said to the acolyte, begging for employment. He was ready to help sew patches on caftans if that was all he was offered.

'The Shepherd is not required to do anything.'

'Why not?'

'The Book says so. Never question the Book.'

'But what do the others do?'

'They receive instruction; rehearse the chants; make things and mend them. That is their work.'

'And what is my work?'

'You are the Shepherd. Go back to your Hut.'

He went back to the Hut and waited for the next service, when for half an hour he was allowed to come to life in the Rite of the Shepherd.

It was truly a rite of Standing. The Shepherd stood. The priest paced about the sanctuary, the acolyte chanted and swung a censer, and a group of girls, the Handmaidens, walked up and down the steps at intervals, singing in high, unmuscular voices, and waving garlands. While all this was going on, the little band of players, known as the Consort, circled the well of the temple, punctuating the ceremony with fitful discords. Even tuneless Hanno would have hesitated to call it music. First came the bagpiper, with a mangy sac lodged under his arm like an asthmatic parasite, and after him the fiddler, scraping his single string; then the unspeakable dribbling flautist, and last the drummer, his tabor slung about his neck like a badge of shame. Round and round they went, in and out of the colonnade, weaving and wheezing.

The Shepherd stood.

Besides having nothing to do, he had nothing to say. All the talking was done on his behalf, by the priest. First he stood at the head of the steps, and the people called upon him to hear them, while he poked and peered, trying to make out Ivo's face or his father's; but if they were there he could not see so far and he had to turn away unsatisfied. Then he stood at the altar and the priest called upon the god, in his name. He faced the well, he faced the Hut, he faced the colonnade, he faced the altar, and that was all he did.

One day, however, he observed that he was not alone in his standing. On the other side of the altar a ragged puppet mimed a grotesque reflection of his movements, like the distorted image in the back of a spoon. When the priest bowed the knee or raised his arms, so was Hanno bound to bow the knee and raise his arms, and when he looked over the altar, sure enough, there was the puppet folding and jerking, head askew and mouth agape. It was the madman, Aram.

As soon as the ritual was completed and his stint of standing done, Hanno retired to the Robing Room as usual and allowed the acolyte to relieve him of the vestments. He knew that when he came out the temple would be empty, but for once he was more glad than sorry. He shrugged the sheepskin over his head and stood back to await the acolyte's inevitable valediction.

'Go now to your Hut, Shepherd.'

Hanno decided to risk everything.

'Does the Book say I must?'

The acolyte, on the verge of delivering his stock reply, faltered.

'Well; no. But it's customary.'

'Good.' Hanno turned briskly and walked to the door. 'Then I won't.'

'But the Shepherd always goes to the Hut.'

'Not today.'

He closed the door on the acolyte's protests (Once you would have been cast into a pit and stoned...), turned his back on the path to the sanctuary gate, mallow, lily, spurge, clover, and set out in the other direction, towards the shadowed place behind the altar, calling softly as he walked: 'Aram. Aram?'

When, as a child, he had stood in the well, he had assumed that the altar was at the back of the sanctuary, but in fact it was in the middle. What looked like a wall was only the end of light. The altar had a light side and a dark side. Did the god too have a light side and a dark side; two faces, one looking towards the sun, the other towards the shadow? In spite of Dow's disclaimer, might not Aram indeed be the Ritual Maniac; the Shepherd's dark side, who stood before the dark face of the god, Hanno's other self?

'Aram? Aram!'

He looked back, towards the sanctuary that he had left behind. He supposed that in fact he was still in it, but he felt as though he had stepped from day into night. On the other side of the altar the tiles were striped with bright bars of sunlight. Here where he stood the flowers lay dead under dust. The sun never shone on the hindside of the god. The very dust was cold.

Hanno, accustomed to keeping his tackle, if not himself, in good order, was faintly disgusted. Much as he disliked the temple it was at least alive with purpose; this sunless hinterland was nothing but a rubbish heap. All the refuse of centuries was here, stacked behind curtains turned colourless by dirt. Great cobwebs hung down like fishing nets. Tapestries, larded with filth, clung to the walls by what agency he could not guess. Stacks of wood, too damp to burn, were consumed by rot where fire would never take hold; smashed hurdles, candlesticks, broken doors; a grinning inverted head, knocked from a statue; a bundle of staves like a giant's faggot. Altar vessels, shattered beyond repair, lay among sheepskins grizzled with age and cracked on the leather side. And flowers. Everywhere, dead flowers.

A man lived here.

'Aram! Aram!'

He searched, blinded by dust; stumbling, choking, spitting.

'*Aram!*'

Against a distant column a torch burned in a bracket. He fetched it down and held it at arm's length and the smoky flame showed him at once what the dark had denied him; one of the rubbish heaps was inhabited. Raising the torch he stooped and looked into the mouth of the burrow. He saw a bed of rags and a broken basket, a chipped flagon with the handle gone, a little pyre of withering roses and a bundle of dried reeds. Aram had made for himself a hut, like the Shepherd's Hut, of splintered hurdles and broken staves. Instead of a tent-cloth it was roofed with the remains of a tapestry. An oil lamp lay in one corner. Hanno imagined that Aram perhaps lay in bed at times, on his back as Hanno did, and looked upwards to the roof of his hut. He raised the torch as high as he dared without setting fire to the tapestry, and saw that Aram had a picture to look at. It was not a picture that Hanno would have cared to lie and look at. Age and dirt had rotted the fabric and fibres, eroded the colours, erased the design, but there was enough left to show him that the scene portrayed was that of a sacrifice; the ritual death of a ram. The beast sat back on its haunches, forced there by the man who stood behind it, his fingers entwined in the fleece at the back of its neck. In his other hand, upraised, he held a knife, the point of the blade directed towards the ram's straining throat. The workmanship was crude and the animal's head had weathered away to a scrub of frayed threads, but there remained a single eye, disturbingly human, and a crimped spiral that must be a horn.

And he lies there and looks at it.

Then he looks at me. Hanno lowered the torch and backed out of the hovel. His fingers touched toes. Claws? Toes.

He looked up. There stood Aram. In the torch's light Hanno saw him clearly for the first time, animated rags and bones and garlanded with a foul wreath of the same dead flowers that littered the dust. Hanno recognized them as a parody of the tiles on the floor; rose, lily, woodbine, mallow, hemlock. He carried a broken besom that had moulted all but a few twigs, as Hanno carried the staff.

Aram showed no displeasure at discovering a trespasser in his precinct. He looked at Hanno from under his hair which came out of his head like straw escaping from a torn mattress.

‘The worm cometh up,’ he said conversationally.

‘Me?’ Hanno thought he was being personal. He stood up and hastened to explain his errand. ‘I came to ask you – if you would not – mock – me, when I stand at the altar.’ Aram nodded, helpfully. ‘I feel enough of a fool as it is.’

‘It is written in the Book that the day of the worm cometh,’ said Aram. ‘Who shall see it?’

‘Please: don’t make fun of me. We can be friends. . .’

‘I shall rise like a cloud at dawn, and you shall sink like a stone,’ said Aram, not smugly, but with conviction.

Hanno wondered how long it had been before anyone realized that Aram was mad. To his unsympathetic ears Aram’s remarks sounded no crazier than anything else he had heard in the last few days. But only a madman would choose to live face to face with that fearful picture. Aram dived past him and burrowed into his frowzy den. He looked over his shoulder at Hanno.

‘Remember, Shepherd. The sky shall open like the mouth of the basilisk on that day. All men shall see it.’ He drew the edge of the tapestry across the opening. He at least could shut his front door.

The Handmaidens had their own hall where they lived and took their meals. They had their own pool and their own chaperone, a repellent lady, built like a menhir and about as impressionable. For much of the day they stayed behind the row of closed doors, but at times they came out in a flock, like pigeons, and settled like pigeons in the garden or the courtyard, round the rim of the fountain.

Hanno, having freed himself from the confines of the Hut, began to prowl. No lover of crowds, he found that he wanted company now that he could not have it, but all he got was Dow who came at him moralizing, like an elderly virgin aunt. At meals he was ignored, in spite of his most amiable overtures. He walked in the courtyard, from group to group, Handmaidens or Guardians or both, hoping to be detained. He was acknowledged, courteously even, but not detained. He was prepared to talk; not prepared to be the first to speak in case he was answered: Go back to your Hut, Shepherd.

Among the girls he saw Nola, who had sat by the fountain stoning flowers, and snubbed him on the day that he was chosen. Unwilling to court another snub he watched her from a distance, seeing little but knowing that she turned her head away and smiled. No hope there. Egil radiated cold disdain. No hope there. Some wove baskets, plaited garlands or stitched embroidery. Some set up skittles, threw quoits, played at cup and ball. They were absorbed. No hope there.

In one corner of the garden the musicians gathered to rehearse. They did not encourage an audience and sat in a tight circle, hunched over their instruments, as though jealously guarding a secret. Hanno thought that if they needed to conceal anything it was their ineptitude, but contempt was poor consolation. No hope there.

Nola had a friend, a cushiony girl called Cariola, whose brainless bulk she used as a foil for her own slender wit. Cariola, unaware, wallowed in her wake, a bolster stood on end, draped in white veiling and rippling all over with downy giggles. She was as kind as she was stupid, full of ruth and charity, and inevitably she began to feel sorry for Hanno. He noticed her because she reminded him a little of Anise, or of two Anises rolled together, and he knew that she was sorry before she did, bracing himself for the moment when she would do something about it. She ran him to earth in a dark corner where he couldn't get out.

'Shepherd, why are you so unhappy?' He was sufficiently acute to observe that although she addressed him by his title, she was talking to him, not to the Shepherd.

'I'm lonely,' he said shortly. 'What do you think?'

He doubted very much if she did think, but she was all feeling.

'You mustn't be lonely.' Her lip, and everything round it, trembled. 'How can you be lonely with so many of us here?'

'But I'm not with you, am I?' he said. 'No one will speak to me.' He sounded to himself like a child clamouring for affection. Nobody loves me. Well, nobody did.

'There's no point in talking to you, they say. You don't listen.'

'I do.'

'They say you won't take advice.'

'Who advises me?'

'Everyone. But you don't take any notice – they say. We want to help you and you won't let us.'

He thought, She's got this by heart. Who drilled her; Dow?

He said, 'Help? I don't want help. I want to talk.'

Cariola's face fell as far as it could, which was not very far, being buoyed up with chins. 'We want to be your Friends.'

That's Dow.

'Be friendly, then.'

'All right.' She smiled generously, spreading all round the smile like a jellyfish. 'Come with me now to the garden.'

And that's not Dow. That's Cariola. That's her own invitation – not at all what Dow would like. What will happen if I accept?

'And if I come? Will they all turn their backs?'

'No. Not if you come with me.'

I wonder. 'Then I will.'

The corner was so full of Cariola that he feared to move in case he struck some vulnerable promontory. He was ready to agree to anything if she would only let him out.

'Come, then. Come now.' She held out her hand, quilted with dimples, which he did not take; but he followed. They crossed the well of the temple. Hanno walked. Cariola trundled. He wondered if she had any feet under the upholstery. As they reached the colonnade a dusty cry floated after them.

'Shepherd.'

'That's Aram,' said Cariola, accelerating down the steps.

'I know.' He followed her.

'Shepherd!'

He went on down.

'Shepherd!'

And down.

'Shepherd!'

He looked round. Aram had not come after him; he was where he usually stood, by the altar. It was his voice that had come in pursuit, like a retrieving hound sent after a fugitive. Louder, and yet more insistent, it howled about his head.

'Shepherd!'

He thought he saw the nearest Guardian permit himself a smile of derision. Would he be the more derided if he went back or if he went on? Aram would keep the hound at his heels. He went back.

'Don't wait,' he said to Cariola, who clearly had no intention of coming with him. No one sought Aram's company. 'I'll catch you up.'

Cariola looked sorrier than ever and hurried away. Hanno returned to the altar.

'How do the god come to you, Shepherd? In the sun at noon or the rain of evening?' said Aram. In his hands he held a sand clock, balanced between his palms, and the sand, half at one end and half at the other, surged in two timeless traps as he tilted it. 'The god is in the sand,' said Aram. 'On that day, it will run and run.'

'I know,' said Hanno, fearing that with Aram, as with everyone else, argument was the rocky road to disaster.

'Remember it,' said Aram. 'On that day, remember it.'

He put the sand clock on the altar and picked up a vase, very similar to the one that Ivo had so admired on the night of the Festival. From the recesses of his wrappings he drew out a rag and began to polish the pot. It was made of unglazed earthenware.

'See how it shines,' said Aram. The matt surface of the pot became felted over with a coarse white lint as the cloth rasped against it. 'It is a remnant of the god's garment,' Aram said, and held up the pot to his face, as if admiring his reflection in it. Hanno, visited by the discomforting thought that perhaps Aram *could* see his reflection in it, backed away before Aram decided to see anything else. Proceeding gingerly across the sanctuary, spurge, aconite, lily, he wondered how far he would get before Aram set the dog on him again, but the madman was engrossed in his work; breathing on the pot, rubbing it with the cloth, and holding it up appraisingly to the light.

The sun was small and high over the garden. Little fearless insects hovered about the flowers and the lawn blossomed with young girls, pink and golden, with garlands spread across their laps. Their lives were all flowers, inside the temple and out, rose, lily, clover, daisy. When he came in at the gate, all their faces turned at once, like heliotropes looking towards the sun. Among them sat Egil and Dow, unarmed but not at all disarmed. Up got Cariola, rosy with pleasure. She took his unready hand and pulled him towards the group on the grass.

'Here's the Shepherd,' she said, redundantly, for they had all seen him. Even here he was still the Shepherd.

'Call me Hanno,' he pleaded.

'Sit down, won't you, Shepherd,' said Nola, and two or

three of them made room for him on the turf. When he sat, they petted him gently as though he were a restless dog that needed to be pacified and settled. He looked at Nola, but she kept her hands in her lap and knitted her fingers into the stems of her garland. The intrusive caressing of the others irritated him, but irritated him less than her reluctance to touch him. She disliked him. How could she not like him without knowing him? She sat toe to sandaled toe with Egil. That was how.

'Why are you here, Shepherd?' said Egil.

'Isn't it allowed? I was invited...' He looked round, knocked off balance by Egil's unseasonable hostility. 'Cariola...?'

'You told him to come?' said Egil. Cariola looked frightened, ready to deny everything.

'Not today. I said he might come, but not today, I didn't say he might –'

'Does the Book forbid me?' said Hanno, wishing himself back in the Hut before anyone could order him there. Dow, all earnest evangelism, leaned forward.

'Of course not. You aren't a prisoner. But we would have thought that you wouldn't yet be ready to leave the sanctuary. Usually the Shepherd fears to go very far from the altar in the early days.'

'I should be afraid?'

'Are you not? You are still very young in this life. Has the god spoken to you already?'

'Yes,' said Hanno, staring him out. 'He told me not to be afraid.'

'Very clever,' said Egil, under his breath. 'But not clever enough.' He raised his voice. 'Do you think it pleases the god when you turn your back and walk away from his presence? You are his servant, not his friend. If you came from such a good family you must have had servants?'

'Yes.'

'And did they not fear you?'

Hanno smiled at the thought of anyone fearing him. 'I hope not. No, of course they didn't.'

'All the same, if you ordered them to wait on you, you would not expect them to walk away, to amuse themselves?'

'I never ordered them to do anything,' said Hanno, unable to describe adequately the ambiguous position he had occupied at home. He felt he was on to the winning argument, however.

'But if you had ordered them? Would they have turned their backs?'

'Quite likely, if it was a silly order. They aren't stupid, our servants.'

'But then, you aren't a god,' said Egil. 'You admit that your servants were cleverer than you –'

'No!'

'You aren't suggesting, I suppose, that you are cleverer than the god?'

'No.'

'If you were fool enough to be despised by your servants, then you deserved their contempt. Now you are the servant.'

Hanno looked round. The placid little faces had become perturbed, regarding him unhappily as though he were the author of their distress. Whether or not they were aware of the extent of Egil's nasty temper, he was the one who had aroused it. He was the stranger, the discordant note that spoiled peaceful music.

'You think I should go back?'

'I? Even a servant can think for himself.'

In came Dow again, beady-eyed. 'If you are not yet at ease in the presence of the god, running away won't help.'

'I wasn't running away.'

'Then why are you here?' said Egil. 'If I leave my post, then I have run away. Why should it be different for you?'

Nola looked up at last and spoke.

'He doesn't want to be Shepherd. He wants to be Hanno. That's the difference.'

'Can't I be both?' His frustration was beginning to hurt for it seemed to him terribly cruel that he should be not only shut in but shut out, too. Guardians or Handmaidens, they were still people with their own names. They had reduced him to the position of a coat-hanger, something to carry the sacred vestments; a thing, indistinguishable from all the other things that had gone before him, and all those that would come after him. His ritual staff was of more significance than he was.

'Why not have a wooden Shepherd, too?' he burst out.

'I thought we had,' said Nola. 'Go back to your Hut, Shepherd.'

'No.'

'I'll come with you,' said Dow, as if he had not spoken.

'No.'

'And I'll come with you,' said Egil. They both stood up and looked down at him where he sat, each standing figure a silent challenge to his refusal to stand, and then, as if in response to an unheard signal, they all stood and left him alone, dreadfully diminished, on the grass.

He intended to stay there for as long as they cared to wait, and gazed up at them, his jaws locked tight with rage and a rogue muscle tugging at the corner of his mouth; but officious Dow must lean down and put a hand under his elbow to pull him to his feet. He wrenched his arm away and stood unaided, and instantly staggered as if pole-axed – as he very nearly was – by a brilliant pain that clouted him across the eyes. For a moment he could only stand, gasping, with his palms pressed to his disintegrating head.

'Have you a headache?' said one concerned voice.

A headache? A needle stabbed him first in the right eye, then in the left, drawing after it a fiery thread that pulled tighter and finer, vibrant, and he thought that he screamed such a scream that the whole world must hear it and fear it, except that his mouth never opened and the scream was all in his head, on one single shrilling note between his eyes.

The thread broke, the pain and his anger with it. He felt something warm run down his arm.

He looked then, and saw blood. His nose was bleeding.

'Oh look. His nose is bleeding,' said the same comfortable, mundane voice that had identified his headache. It could only be Cariola, solidly untouched by everything that had happened. She was happy, because she could do something for him. He was pulled down again, handled, surrounded, and knelt with his hands over his face and the blood running between his fingers, cowering among them. They were all going to do something for him. They were his Friends, after all, and he had made it very difficult for them to help him. Now they were going to help him, whether he liked it or not.

He survived the noonday service, in mortal dread that his nose would bleed again, but he discovered, in that short time, that fear would only help him. It was anger that had struck him down, and might strike him down again. Fear would remind him that anger was his enemy. Fear would make him become willing. He went to the Robing Room, left the vestments with the acolyte, and went willingly to his Hut where he lay on the fringed blanket, blessedly alone. Now that he had Friends he didn't want them. He stroked his nose tenderly, as if it were a small hurt animal that had come to him for comfort, and suffered, with something very like relief, the hollow soreness behind his eyes that was the shadow of that earlier agony. The fear came from the knowledge that he had brought it on himself. Hanno had hurt Hanno, for the sake of the Shepherd, because the Shepherd must become willing.

He managed to sleep for a while and when he woke he saw that the sun had fallen below the wall and it was time to dress again for the last service of the day. When he stood up, his head felt enormously light and empty, all the weight under his eyes. He could only imagine what he looked like, pallid as a toadstool with black bruises staining his cheekbones. At the door of the Robing Room he paused to think about this. He could only imagine, because there was no way of finding out. There were no mirrors.

'Have you a mirror?' he asked the acolyte, Master of the Robes, when the sheepskin was on him, the belt about his waist, the horns upon his head.

'What for do you want a mirror?' said the acolyte.

'To see myself in,' said Hanno.

'Why should you want to do that?'

'Why not?'

The acolyte put his face between the horns and addressed him in tones of rebuke.

'Your appearance is of no concern to you now. When you put on the head-dress you are the Shepherd. The face beneath is nothing.'

Nothing. Now determined to find his reflection Hanno strode out of the Robing Room and went, not to the sanctuary but through the slype to the bath house. Above him the open sky was ribbed with pink clouds; at his feet the water reflected the ribs, cross-hatched with ripples. When he leaned down to look he saw a shuddering silhouette, but no features. The cistern was fed by a spring, trapped in a stone channel and liberated through a ram's-horn spout, and the surface trembled continuously. A second silhouette formed beside his own. A hand clasped the fleece upon his shoulder.

'What are you doing here, Shepherd?' It was Dow. For

a moment he had thought it was Aram, and tensed himself against a possible shove that might send him in, head first. But Aram was no more likely to push him in the tank than was Dow.

And no less.

He eased himself from under the hand and stood up. Smiled.

'I felt so sick, I wondered how I looked.'

'Are you sure you didn't want to see how you looked in the Vestments?' Dow didn't show any particular concern for Hanno's sickness, and his hand remained fixed in the fleece. 'It would be a very natural curiosity,' he said.

'No,' said Hanno, more or less truthfully.

'When you put on those Vestments you are no longer Hanno, you are the Shepherd. The people do not see you, they see the Shepherd.'

'But they know who I am; some of them.'

'They don't care. They do not think about you. Neither should you think about you. Think only of the Shepherd.'

With what he probably took to be unobtrusive firmness, he was slowly pushing Hanno towards the door, back to the slype, through the slype, into the temple, lily, spurge, mallow, aconite, rose. There he left him.

Hanno waited until the door of the Guardians' hall had closed behind him and set off round the sanctuary, towards the colonnade. Before he reached it Nola accosted him, not with a hand, but simply by crossing his path and defying him to advance another step.

'Where are you going, Shepherd?'

'What's it to you?' He had been going to the fountain, the one other mirror that he knew of.

'You cannot go out of the Temple when you are wearing the Vestments. That would be sacrilege. The Holy Garments may be worn only in the Holy Place. Go back, Shepherd.'

He looked over her head to the fountain. Beyond, the gate stood open and the faithful came in by it. If only the faithless could go out.

'Go back, Shepherd.' She made a little pushing movement, staying her hands before they could come close enough to touch him, so that she seemed to be warding him off. Incensed, he stepped forward; she stepped back, and immediately two of those Guardians who stood with their faces turned away, seeming to see nothing, crossed their spears and made a barrier: on the outside, Nola; on the inside, Hanno.

He stared at her, across the barrier, petrified with fury. He was ready to sweep the spears aside and stride between, felling Nola if she did not make way for him, trampling on her because he could not go where he wanted to go. Just in time he felt the warning tremor between the eyes, the first fine filament of pain, and he turned away, and went back, arrested by the brake that gave him pause to think before he spoke.

His old nurse would have called it intelligence.

PART TWO

The Cold Seasons

6

A FAMILY of swallows lodged on a beam beneath the roof, and quested for insects above the courtyard, all through summer; but one day the nest was empty and the birds had gone. Flowers fell from the vines. On the lawn, here and there, a frail toadstool raised its parasol against the cooling sun. In the temple the tiles turned cold underfoot as the daylight withdrew daily. In the courtyard one morning, the Shepherd stood at the foot of the wall, as he so often did, and the wind dropped a withered leaf into his hand as if it were a secret message flung over from the city outside. He stayed there for a long time, smoothing the leaf between his fingers, until the dry membrane powdered away leaving only the veins and the stem, like a second hand in his hand. Autumn was happening without him.

He went slowly back to the temple, up the steps, across the tiles, clover, spurge, mallow, rose, more steps, more tiles, and into the Hut, where he laid the skeleton on the table among his other possessions; a letter from his father, full of loving congratulations, and a letter from Ivo. Ivo's letter upset him every time he read it, which was more often than he wanted to. He had to conserve his sight and his patience, both of which were beginning to fail him. Folded and smoothed and refolded until it was as lacy as a dead leaf, it yielded him nothing, no matter how often he looked at it. The Ivo who had written these lines was no longer the man who had promised to pray that Hanno would not become the Ritual Shepherd. The words were a clumsy attempt to conceal transparent joy, and as he read them he knew without doubt that Ivo had hoped very much that his brother would be chosen. Hanno cast his mind back to their last conversation on the Mill Bridge; to Ivo's painful fears for his future and his opinion that it would do Hanno no harm to learn to hold his tongue.

You should see how I hold it, Hanno thought. He wished that Ivo would come and see him. No matter how often, how courteously he asked, he was not allowed to go and see Ivo.

In three months only two letters, but in fact he had written only one himself. *Dear Father*, *Dear Ivo*, *I am the Shepherd*. . .There was nothing more to say; nothing more that he could safely say. He suspected that his one letter had been read by alien eyes before it ever reached his home, as he suspected with equal certainty that his family's letters had been read before they reached him. True, he could write quite openly and ask Ivo to visit him, but he refused to ask. Ivo should have come without asking. He should have known that his brother must be wretchedly unhappy and if he declined to know, Hanno declined to tell him, finding a shred of comfort in his miserable pride.

The temple bell was cracked and could only utter a muted blah-blah-blah, in the querulous voice of an old sheep. It rang first at dawn and roused Hanno to face a grey morning with no promise of sunshine. He turned his head and looked out through his doorway, trying to think of a good reason for getting up. When he had first come to the temple the sun had risen swiftly above the wall to beckon him out, but by now it was late morning before it showed itself, and when the sky was cloudy he remained supine, staring at the sagging tent-cloth and listening for the advancing footsteps of the sanctuary cleaner; refusing to move until only seconds separated him from the shock of a wet mop shoved in his face. It was no part of the cleaner's job to waken him but she enjoyed doing it. He usually managed to forestall her. It was his own method of getting himself up: the pleasure of denying her the pleasure.

This morning he heard no footsteps. Perhaps the old bitch had dropped dead at her bucket, or gasped her last horrible gasp during the night. He sat up and looked round the edge of the hurdles; there was no one about. His finely tuned ears picked up a faint snore from Aram's distant den, clattering dishes behind the closed doors of the cookhouse, small clicks and clanks as a watchful Guardian eased his cold limbs, but no rattling bucket; no footsteps. He was very tempted to lie down again, but an early riser could be certain of a solitary visit to the bath house, and he was beginning to love solitude as he had never loved it before. Sometimes he found himself trapped in there with a whole platoon of Guardians refreshing themselves after a turn on duty, and then he stood, at best nervous at worst afraid, on the narrow slippery ledge that lay round the tank, and felt himself submerged before he even entered the water. He got up.

It was still too dull to see the flowers beneath his feet but his educated toes discovered the path that he trod daily; rose, mallow, lily, hemlock, clover, aconite, lily, rose. That took him to the sanctuary gate. He knew better now than to step over the railing. Through deeper shadow he made his way to the bath house, sorrel, woodbine, clover, sorrel, aconite, mallow, rose, hemlock, spurge. The black clear scent of water in the slype made him think of the river, the image intensified by the rebellious murmuring of the rivulet that fed the cistern. He had lived by the river all his life and never wasted a moment on thoughts of drowning. What was happening to him? He wondered what had happened to his boat, and to his other Anise. The boat would wait for him, but would she?

There was over an hour to go before the morning service, an event that became less of an event as the few early worshippers, discouraged by their own depleted numbers, became fewer. Hanno felt, obscurely, that this was in some way his fault, as if his faithlessness had infected their faith. More rationally, he doubted that this was possible. As he had been told, over and over again, the people saw the Shepherd, they did not see Hanno, and the Shepherd's distant, disguised figure could tell them nothing about the man beneath the head-dress. And he did his best for them, and for the temple. Once he would have spent that spare hour in the Hut; now he understood that the Shepherd was a symbol, and without significance unless he was seen. He went to the altar, kneeled down, and raised his arms in supplication before the god who was not there.

Even Egil, if he looked now, would see the Shepherd at his prayers and be satisfied. Dow was easily satisfied. It was simple enough to deceive a fanatic; less simple to fool the sceptic, Egil. Being naturally mistrustful he had to mistrust someone, and he had elected Hanno.

Hanno's arms began to ache, as manual labour had never made them ache, but he forced himself to keep them at full stretch until he had counted slowly to five hundred. He adhered to a strict time-table. Knowing that he could not remain kneeling for very long he had calculated that he could look even more submissive by prostrating himself at intervals. Groaning a little, as he had heard devout old women groan, he slid forward, prayerfully, until he lay with his forehead supported on the trestles of his knuckles. Flowers blossomed before his eyes, and, if he looked too long, faded and died.

Like this he counted to a thousand, then it was time to move before someone fancied he had fallen asleep; before he really did fall asleep. He knelt again, cupping his hands over his face, and hidden in the red cave he heard the temple stir itself, identifying each sound, each footstep; the restless animal sound of something coming awake on straw, an inarticulate muttering, snore and snort. Looking through the lancets between his fingers he saw the altar loom like a cliff in front of him. Arranged on top of it, among the sheepskins and each in its designated place, stood the massive earthenware vessels, sacred utensils that had no use. As he watched, a thin grey arm rose like smoke from behind the altar, a hand closed round the slender neck of a portly vase and lifted it down, out of sight.

Aram.

Dow was eating an onion. Hanno, who disliked onions and was beginning to detest them, watched with nauseated fascination as he dipped it into a bowl of salt and gnawed it down to the root. He felt his own throat close up with every mouthful until he was unable to finish his own meal. Dow didn't seem to be enjoying it much, either, and it was his third that week.

'Why do you do it?' Hanno asked, when Dow finally managed to ingest the last mouthful.

'To Mortify myself,' said Dow, with some difficulty, but a certain amount of pride.

'I can see that,' Hanno said. 'Why do you? No one else does.'

Dow glanced at the water jug but resisted temptation. 'We all do, at some time or another. If the Priest thinks we need to Subdue the Spirit he urges us to eat the Bread of Mortification.'

'But it's not bread.'

'It is in memory of the Great Famine, as the Book tells us. It is written in the Book that the god took pity upon the starving and sent a miraculous crop of onions to save the city.'

'He would have done better to send bread.'

'So now,' Dow continued, ignoring him, 'we eat onions to Remind ourselves of the Great Suffering and at the same time of the god's Goodness.'

'How come you have to eat so many?' said Hanno, who had assumed that Dow's priggish piety would be looked on with favour by the priest. 'Does your spirit need so much subduing?'

Dow looked quite disgracefully puffed up. 'I have never yet been *ordered* to eat the Bread of Mortification,' he said, modestly. 'But I know that my Spirit needs to be Subdued. I choose to subdue it. Likewise my Flesh, as does yours, I don't doubt. You should eat one,' he said.

'I don't think I could,' said Hanno.

'You could if you were told to,' said Egil, behind him. Hanno had not noticed him lingering at the next table. 'You'd get it down, somehow.'

That evening, when he went in to supper, he found on his trencher a monstrous vegetable, the grandmother of all onions, squatting malevolently in a hoarfrost of salt.

You bastard, he thought, looking round at Egil who was looking round at him.

'What's this for?' he said, aloud.

'To subdue the spirit,' said Egil. 'Perhaps the priest thinks that your prayers lack humility.'

After all that crawling about on the floor?

'He didn't say anything to me.'

'Why should he say anything to you? If you are sent the Bread of Mortification, you eat it. We all know that.'

'I can't eat it,' Hanno said, flatly.

'You can't refuse,' said Dow. 'Not if the Priest sent it.'

'I know who sent it, and it wasn't the priest.'

'You won't get anything else until you have eaten it,' said Egil, and turned back to his table. Hanno and the onion looked at each other. The onion leered. Hanno felt tears gathering at the corners of his eyes as it breathed venomous gases in his face, and he hurriedly lowered his head until his hair hung down and hid him, in case anyone thought he was weeping. Egil, you toad, you louse, you scrofulous son of a sow, I swear I'll tear your infested head from your scrawny neck and boil it in a cast-iron cooking pot, he whispered. He raised his eyes, took one last look at the onion's implacable, sweaty stare, and fled from the table.

'It'll still be there in the morning,' Egil called after him, as he reached the door. 'And it'll be a whole day older!'

The sanctuary lamp hung high above the altar and shed no light, one more star among the many that studded the ring of round windows in the clerestory over the colonnade. Hanno went to the Hut where he lay on the couch and waited for sleep to release him from duty. But the onion haunted him; resentment rose up and battled with boredom; he lay awake and grew increasingly resentful the more sleepless he became. His head began to ache.

He mistrusted Egil quite as much as Egil mistrusted him. Dow was nominally the leader of the Guardians, but Hanno guessed that he had no control over Egil. Egil controlled himself, using the ritual as a text-book. Who controlled the priest? Only one person in this place could be thought of as a free agent; Aram.

Sooner or later Aram was going to come out from behind the altar and creep towards the Hut, unerring in the dark, with a mouth full of debatable revelations. As insubstantial as the air he seemed to feed on he haunted Hanno like a devoted ghost, because Hanno was the Shepherd and had the ear of the god.

Once he had hoped that this might set him apart, lend him distinction; not because he valued distinction but because it would have given him a base from which to defend himself. He was defenceless. It was the people from whom he was set apart; in the temple he felt himself despised and knew Egil as the root of that contempt. Between Aram's devotion and Egil's contempt there was only pity. Cariola.

At the thought of Cariola the headache surged forward

and broke against his forehead like a wave. Cariola knew all about his headaches and studied his face for signs of them, like an astrologer looking for disasters in the sky. She was waiting for him to have another nose-bleed so that she could cure it as she had cured the first, holding him down with his head between her terrible nutcracker knees while he struggled and choked in deathly fear of drowning. In fact there had been two more since then, each worse than the one before, but no one knew except Aram. Aram had come upon him last time, changing his tunic afterwards; had observed him silently and then remarked: 'You bleed in the face, Shepherd,' as though it were a detail that might have escaped Hanno's attention.

An unheard movement stirred the air and set the sanctuary lamp swinging on the end of its chain. Hanno propped himself on one elbow and drew up his feet, ready to twist aside at the moment of contact. Aram was certain to introduce himself by laying a hand on Hanno's cheek and Hanno, who was learning to shrink from the most harmless human touch, was profoundly distressed at the prospect of Aram's clammy palm plastered across his face. A moment before the hand came coldly out of the dark he rolled over and the probing fingers went deep into the fringe of the blanket that lay over his shoulder.

'God has visited you with a beard, Shepherd,' said Aram, hoarsely. 'It is the beard of an old man on a young man's face.'

'It's the blanket, you fool,' said Hanno, pushing him away.

'A beard groweth upon the face of the young man, and the old man's face shall be as smooth as sand.'

'Go away. Go and sleep. Let me sleep.'

Aram took no notice of him. He liked sand. The temple masons, carrying out much-needed repairs at the back, had left a heap of sand in the courtyard and Aram was transfering the heap, handful by handful, to his den, but it was slow work.

'*Will* you get out?'

'The day of the worm cometh, and the sand shall run and run through the glass on that day...'

'Go to bed, Aram, please.'

'And I shall be taken up...'

A slithering as soft as the passage of a snake, a passing eclipse of the stars, and Aram had gone, taking his vision with him. Hanno lay down again, on his back, and stared at the stars until they turned to elder-flowers floating on the surface of the night. Worms... ?

The Onion was waiting for him at breakfast, unmoved since their last encounter. Egil was on duty in the colonnade; the Onion was his viceroy, sent to remind the Shepherd of his subjection to the Book. Hanno stood in the doorway, under the eyes of the entire company, and exchanged a long, loathing look with the Onion. Someone laughed. He went out again, slamming the door.

He stumbled through the morning service, yawning, scarcely aware of the little puddle of worshippers in the well of the temple and convinced that the Onion was somewhere about, fuming vilely. When he returned to the Hut, after the service, he found it sitting on the table beside his couch. He buried his nose in the crook of his arm and turned his back on the beast. He was no longer hungry.

'Get it over with,' Dow advised, stooping in at the doorway of the Hut. 'Eat it now. It won't improve with keeping.'

'I can't.'

'Everyone must at some time.'

'I suppose Egil put it in here. Well, didn't he?'

'Why must you think of Egil as your enemy?' said Dow. 'He is stern, but not unjust.'

'Who's he to decide if my spirit needs subduing?'

'Well, doesn't it?'

'Yes,' said Hanno, realizing that he couldn't possibly say no. He was quite certain that Dow had dropped in to make sure that he ate the Onion. Dow was an expert at eating Onions. He ate them from choice. Hanno would only eat his when he had despaired of disposing of it any other way. He yawned again. He was close to falling asleep and he would have leaned against the wall of the Hut, only he feared that the hurdles would collapse and he would somersault backwards off the couch.

Dow was scraping at a little pile of sand on the floor.

'Aram's been here?'

'Last night.'

'And what's he seen this time?' Dow, like everyone else, followed his own advice about laughing at Aram. This did not prevent him from laughing when Aram was elsewhere.

'He thinks I've grown a beard,' said Hanno. Dow's smile became slightly superior, and Hanno knew what he was thinking. Hanno's beard would have been as dark as his hair but it grew finely and he shaved only three times a week to Dow's seven. Dow was younger but he looked older. Hanno looked like a sheep. End of thought.

'Eat it,' said Dow, prodding the Onion. 'I'll help you.'

'How? By poking it down with a stick?' My god; he might, too.

'I'd Encourage you,' said Dow, but instead of carrying out this fearful threat he stopped mauling the Onion and suddenly changed the subject. 'That head-dress,' he said.

'Yes?' What's that got to do with onions? Let me sleep.

'How much can you hear when you've got it on?'

'Not a lot. Only people near me.'

'Then you don't hear what's going on during the services?'

He's trying to trap me. Now what have I done? 'I hear

the priest, but I stand right next to him. I can't help hearing.' He feared that he sounded ungracious. 'I don't hear the responses.'

'That's what I meant.' Hanno saw that he was not the object of the probing. 'This morning no one could hear the responses. Not even Cariola, and she stands on the steps.'

'Well, I wouldn't know.' During a service his attention was all taken up by his part in the ritual. What went on beyond the sanctuary railing should have been his concern, but it was not. He knew that out there, in the well of the temple, the faithful worshipped, taking their cue from his faithless worship, because he was the Shepherd and they looked on him to lead them. When the priest called to the god in the name of the Shepherd they responded; but had they all remained mutinously mute he would have been none the wiser and cared less.

'I'll tell you why you can't hear the responses.' Dow looked up, angry, as though he had been personally affronted. 'There were so few people that I could have counted them.' He wouldn't have counted them, of course. He would have been too intent on making his own responses. 'Cariola counted them.'

'And how many were there?'

'Twenty-three. Women and old men. Little girls.' Dow looked as if he might spit, but he was inside the sanctuary. 'I've seen hundreds at Morning Service – ten thousand at a Festival. My father brought me to the Temple as soon as I could learn the chants and then we stood shoulder to shoulder, all the men in our street.'

'Did I know you then?' For a moment he saw in Dow's stocky figure the pugilist child. Did Dow remember Hanno as the long-armed little boy who had consistently out-fought him? Perhaps he preferred to forget.

'And this morning; twenty-three, and seventeen of them were women. *Women*.'

So you were counting. Hanno wondered if Dow's dislike of women was the virtue he supposed.

'My father brought me too,' he said, without any nostalgia. He had been a natural-born fidget, bored senseless even then by the monotonous chanting, the sour green twanging of the band, the inactivity. Oh, how hot it had been in summer; how cold and close in winter. So many people, all bigger than he was.

'So you remember how crowded it used to be?' He remembered that as well as anything. The services had been a daily celebration of panic.

'But how we enjoyed it!'

'We did?' He coughed. 'We did.' We? Presumably they had all been there, lost in the press. Dow, Egil, Nola, Cariola; innocent children and even Aram, perhaps, not yet run mad; and up in the sanctuary, year after year, the Shepherd. He did not know when he had first understood that it was not always the same Shepherd. Now they were men in their late twenties and thirties, and he was the Shepherd.

Dow drew his finger through the scattered sand.

'This place is like a midden. No one comes to clean. You can write in the dirt. When was the last time anyone cleaned in here?' Hanno shrugged. It was some days since the sanctuary cleaner had last come at him with her mop and no one had tidied the hut since then. 'They send out the Crier and no one comes. I remember my mother, my aunts, used to put on their best clothes to clean the Temple before a Festival. They would leave the house singing and work all day. They sang at their work. My sisters used to cry because they were too young to go as well.'

'Really?' Hanno was swaying with fatigue. His eyes went out of focus. Possibly Dow's mother and aunts had run singing to the temple because it was a chance to get away from Dow for a bit. No wonder the little girls had cried at being left behind.

'They send missionaries out to foreign lands. They should send missionaries into the city, among our people. If the faith dies, the city dies. We cannot live without it.'

You speak for yourself, thought Hanno, vulgarly. He said, 'Have you mentioned any of this to the priest?'

'He knows. What can he do? He's so old.'

'I should tell him anyway. Go and tell him now,' Hanno urged. *Go.* His head was beginning to ache again, as though Dow were actively boring a hole into his skull. He ground his teeth helplessly. Why should I have to sit here and listen to him? Who does he think he is? He felt a pulse spring to life behind his eyes and his thoughts began to scale the ladder of catastrophe. If I don't get some sleep soon I shall have a real headache, and if I have a real headache my nose will bleed, and if Dow sees it he'll send for Cariola. Oh no, please, not Cariola. He abandoned his efforts to sit upright and dropped on to the couch. Dow poked him.

'The Bread of Mortification.'

He opened his eyes with difficulty. The Onion floated towards him. Levitation? No, Dow was holding it.

'Shepherd! The Bread of Mortification.'

Bugger the Bread of Mortification. 'Dow, take it away, for god's sake. I shall throw up.' The last sound he heard was Dow's angry gasp at the god's name being taken in vain. He slept.

A hand on his face...

Aram was standing by the couch, peering into his eyes and waving the Onion about like a stinking censer.

'One day,' said Aram, chattily, 'the heavens shall open like the mouth of the basilisk.'

One day, thought Hanno, I shall certainly kill one of them. He hid his face in the blanket.

'And mine head shall be cloven like a cheese, and my

spirit shall be taken up out of it, and the cleft shall close and I shall be found with no mark on me.'

'I'm sure you will,' said Hanno, as if quieting an importunate child. It was consoling to think of Aram as an importunate child, otherwise one had to remember that he was demented, which was infinitely less consoling, especially as he had a habit of appearing suddenly with heavy objects in his hand. Just now he was hefting a half-brick, picked up no doubt from the pile of rubble left by the masons. He rubbed it against his sleeve. Perhaps he hoped it would shine. Hanno had discovered that he devoted his days to polishing the altar vessels. Using always the same threadbare cloth which he described as the remnant of the god's garment, he would sit for hours with a vase or a bowl in his lap, entranced by the circular motion of his hand against the pottery. He skulked in his den and waylaid the few passers-by who came behind the altar, but he never stopped polishing. Hanno lifted his head quickly before Aram should decide to drop his brick.

'Are you hungry?' he said, pointing to the Onion.

'The world turns and the wheel turns not,' said Aram. Hanno had never seen him eat anything, although he remembered the munching sound that he had mistaken for rats on the night of his vigil. Was it possible that someone put down food for him at nightfall, as country people left out milk and bread to sustain and appease restless spirits? Aram was certainly a restless spirit, and as incalculable. Those who Dwelt in the Temple regarded him as an accident of nature, like mildew. He was a nuisance, but like any natural phenomenon, he happened, and there was nothing they could do about it. The Book stated that a lunatic was always in the eye of the god.

Aram ignored Hanno's invitation, but after a while he noticed the Onion of his own accord, and began to examine it, as though it had fallen into his hands by supernatural means. Maybe it had; Hanno hadn't actually seen him pick it up.

'You can keep that, if you like,' Hanno said.

'Mortify the flesh,' Aram advised. Under Hanno's incredulous gaze he began to eat the Onion as happily as anyone else would have bitten into an apple.

'May I have a little?' He should at least smell mortified.

'A little mortification shall be your lot,' said Aram, with condescension. He nipped off a very small piece with his thumb-nail and gave it to Hanno.

'I shall rise like a cloud at dawn and you shall sink like a stone.'

'Thank you,' said Hanno. 'Thank you very much.'

'And there shall be no mark on me.' Aram swallowed the remains of the Onion, contented as a suckling babe, and left the Hut, his eyes crossed with the concentration of putting one foot in front of the other. His relationship with the earth was tenuous at the best of times.

7

A SMALL cold rain fell in the courtyard and puddles spread over the uneven grass-grown paving, turning it into a barren landscape of distant lakes, bordered with sedge. During the service the drizzle turned to a deluge. Hanno stood by the altar, glad at last of the sheepskin that warmed his shoulders, while the Handmaidens shivered damply in their veiling and the priest's bare feet turned blue. The Guardians stood at their posts with water streaming over their armour from the defective guttering above their heads. A step backwards would have taken them to shelter, but the Book ordained their positions and there they stayed, glorying in their discomfort. Dow was in the most exposed position of all, yet he lifted his face to the rain and smiled; the same smile, desirous of martyrdom, that he wore when he was subduing the spirit by consuming unbidden onions, or eating salt without water.

Hanno looked bleakly at the dismal panorama, a foretaste surely of the long wet winter to come. He turned to the altar and said, Now, god, make it stop; and was more put out than otherwise when the sun came from behind the clouds to light the path of the few dogged worshippers who were splashing homeward through the puddles. The morning sun held little warmth, but after the midday meal the Friends began to gather in the courtyard. They favoured the garden, but the grass was too wet for sitting about, so instead they perched on the rim of the fountain. Cariola, passing the door of the Robing Room as he came out, invited Hanno to join them. He was invited daily and, being invited, took pleasure in his freedom to decline, but for appearance's sake he had to join them sometimes and it might as well be today, since he could see no one there who was likely to out-manoeuvre him. He slung a caftan over his tunic and followed her out to the fountain.

As he came closer, however, he observed that his untrustworthy eyes had deceived him again. The fountain was not deep but the rain had filled the basin and in spite of the chill air Nola, always conscious of her decorative value, was trailing her fingers in the water. Beside her, sitting also on the rim, was Dow, relieved of his sentry duty but with his caftan tightly fastened, his boots buckled to the knee. He cast a disapproving glance at Hanno in his unlaced tunic, barefoot, and with his caftan hanging negligently from one shoulder.

Hanno sat down a little way from them, where the rim was widest, because he was sometimes visited by the suspicion that it might occur to one of them to push him in. The thought shamed him, but shame did not free him of it. The water was a foot deep at most, but he knew that it was possible to drown in a foot of water; indeed, probable, if someone held you under. He looked into the shallow basin, paved with blue tiles, and saw himself lying there, his head rolling slowly with the motion of the water and his dead hair drifting before his unnoticing eyes.

The rim of the fountain was a broad ledge. He leaned back on his hands and stretched out his feet in front of him. All his weight was now on his wrists. If someone should upset his balance he would fall back into the water; if someone should trip over his feet, for instance, or playfully buffet his shoulder. He drew his feet towards him and hunched forwards, elbows on knees. Dow and Cariola watched his fidgeting with interest. They knew he was never at ease, but lacked the imagination to determine why. Dow thought he felt unequal to his office; Cariola thought he was shy. Egil was probably closer to the truth than anyone but even he doubted no more than the intensity of Hanno's belief; that the belief existed, he never doubted.

Cariola, always anxious to cure his shyness, came at him smiling, all tenderness, all hands, fastening the neck-strings of his tunic, adjusting the caftan and hooking it across his chest, buckling his belt, while he sat frozen, waiting for the drawstring to be drawn too tight, the belt to trap his arms, the firm touch of her fat hands to become a homicidal thrust that would send him down to the blue tiles under the water.

Oh, you fool, you fool, you fool.

Cariola, her attentions completed, took her hands away and sat down beside him. Dow, now the isolated one, moved up and sat on the other side. Under the skirts of the caftan Hanno clung like toadflax to the lip of the ledge and dug his heels into the stonework.

Go away, go away, go away.

Cariola's arm touched his arm. She said, 'You're shivering. Are you cold? You should have something on your feet. Where are your sandals? I'll fetch your sandals.'

'I don't ha-ha-have any sandals,' he managed to say. 'Not since I came. They were taken from me.' The child again, telling tales.

'I think you could have them back now,' said Dow. 'Ask Egil.'

Why should I have to ask?

'You ought to have something on your feet. The pavement is dangerous. It's time someone saw to the pavement – all those sharp edges,' said Dow, the priest's sing-song inflexion creeping into his voice.

'I've cut myself before now, even in sandals,' said Cariola. 'You shouldn't go about with nothing on your feet.' It must be their long exposure to the temple chants that made them speak antiphonally.

'It would have been safe once to go about with nothing

on your feet. Once they would have sent out the Crier and paviours would have come and attended to it,' said Dow, returning to his favourite gripe like a homing wasp.

'Can't the masons do it?' said Hanno, trying to upset the horrible see-saw of complaints of which he seemed to be the pivot.

'They have no sto-one,' said Dow, keening fondly over the outrage.

'I think I'll go and ask Egil for my sandals,' said Hanno, suddenly noting that they had unwittingly offered him the means of escape.

'He's on duty. I'll ask one of the others!' Cariola leaped up, all eager to help, and knocked him flying. He contrived to twist round as he fell and found himself sprawling across the rim of the basin, up to the elbows in water and with his nose an inch from the surface. Dow, laughing, hauled him back. Cariola enveloped him in apologies, enveloped him in Cariola; there was so much of her, and she was so generous with it. Hanno found his way out, forcing a seedy smile on the way.

'Now I shall have to go in,' he said, holding up his arms in their dripping sleeves as an excuse.

'We'll come with you,' said Cariola, contrite and fearing that he might be angry. She was already bulking up beside him again. He sprang away from the ledge, laughing so that they should see he was propelled by nothing more than high spirits, and took off at a run across the courtyard, pursued by Dow's doleful warnings about the dangers of neglected paving stones.

As he was about to bound up the steps to the sanctuary he saw the acolyte happening by the Hut, and with a dozen transgressions on his conscience he veered to the right and made his way round the far side of the railing, sorrel, woodbine, clover, sorrel. . .Dow was right, the tiles were filthy. He was passing behind the altar, which was a mistake. He had forgotten in his confusion who might be there. Aram was squatting in his den, bowed over a deep terracotta bowl which should have stood in the centre of the altar. It was too late to turn back. Hanno trod softly on, hoping that Aram would not raise his head, over cold flowers. . .no sun here. At the back of the altar winter had come already. He was beginning to think that once, perhaps, the altar had faced this way, to the sunless north, and that things had been done upon it the people should not see. He was beginning to think too much. One sick fancy sprang up where another withered; but seeing Aram brought to mind the ancient tapestry, the sacrificial ram. The beast was caught between life and death and Hanno, besides hating the picture, distrusted it for its spurious air of immediacy, when he knew that it must have taken many months to design and stitch.

Lily, hemlock, rose. . .

'Shepherd!'

Hanno sighed and retraced his steps, knowing that if he did not Aram would howl and hoot, or come after him, prophesying at double his usual volume. No one took much notice of Aram's startling forecasts, but they were an embarrassment. And Hanno was dimly sorry for him.

'The worm cometh up,' said Aram, without raising his eyes. 'I see it.'

'Where?'

'All around cometh the worm. Whomsoever hath seen the worm knows the day when it will come. The man who bleeds in the face shall see it.'

Hanno stopped dead. Aram's words were of his own devising and owed nothing to the Book. In fact, they had no relevance to anything outside Aram's own fog-bound mind, but. . .the man who bleeds in the face. . . ?

'Who is this man?' Hanno stooped down and brought his head level with Aram's. Aram looked at him.

'*You* know.'

The audience was at an end. Hanno stood up and walked away, shaken. It was well known that Aram saw only what he wanted to see. When he saw the priest he saw a priest indeed, not a balding old man with a flimsy beard. When he looked at Dow he saw a temple Guardian, not a strait-laced youth obsessed with ceremony. In Cariola he saw a Handmaid of the god, but when he looked at the Ritual Shepherd he saw a man with a bleeding nose. Did he know that there was nothing else to see?

'O hear us,' said the priest.

Hear who? thought Hanno, three paces behind him. He slid his fingers under one horn of the head-dress and lifted it away from his ear. Very faintly he heard scattered voices in the distance.

'O hear us.' A feeble echo in the quiet winter air, it was followed by a volley of hawking. The flautist drew thin complaints out of his thin pipe. The drummer cracked cold fingers across the skin of his tabor. The one-stringed fiddle mewed. The bagpipe had a cough of the lungs and was mercifully silent.

'How many today, Cariola?' said Dow, afterwards.

'Eleven.'

'Soon there will be no one.'

'Except Aram,' said Hanno.

Hanno was indulging in a silly dream in which everyone stopped coming to the temple and in the end the priest shut up shop and they went back to living their own lives. A fault in the dream lay in the fact that he was the only one with another life to lead. The rest of them, priest, acolyte, Guardians, Handmaidens, all were dedicated to the temple for ever, bound by the dead hand of the Book. The Book commanded that they should hold three services a day when there were scarcely enough worshippers to make one worthwhile. The Book commanded that until the solstice no brazier should be lit in the temple. Any sooner and it would be an act of defilement, no matter how cold the season, and already frost lay in the shadows of the courtyard. The Book gave no reasons and no one questioned it. It was the Book that ordered the choosing of the Shepherd, otherwise they would never have tolerated a process so haphazard that it had chosen him. The Book said that the Shepherd must be unwilling.

'Dow?'

'Shepherd?'

'Why is the Shepherd chosen?'

'The Book demands it.'

'Why? You weren't chosen.'

'I was.'

'But you could have refused.'

Dow looked round apprehensively at Cariola, but she was spread out like a junket, abundantly insulated against the cold and half-asleep.

He said, 'The Shepherd must be unwilling. That is, he does not Offer himself. The Shepherd has never Offered himself. He has to be taken.'

'And that makes him unwilling?'

'You should know,' said Dow, unusually flippant. 'You were more unwilling than most. But we said you'd become willing, didn't we? You didn't believe us, but look at you now.'

Look at me now.

'You can read the Book whenever you like,' said Dow. 'Ask the Priest.'

Hanno doubted very much if he could read the Book and had no intention of trying. With that weakness exposed he would never be free of their hands.

'The priest doesn't speak to me.'

'He would if you spoke to him.'

'I spoke to him once. He told me that the Shepherd needs to know nothing.'

'That's a pity,' said Dow, 'because he tells a good story.'

Hanno thought this unlikely. 'What kind of stories?'

'Tales of the old Miracles; of the great Sages. There should be Miracles now,' said Dow. 'That would bring the people back to us.'

Soft footsteps came up behind them. Where Dow's sharp voice had failed to penetrate the padding of bare feet disturbed. Cariola's head jerked up and she looked round, her big harmless mouth compressed into a tiny spout of dismay. Aram stood at the top of the steps. He placed his hand on the nearest head, which was Hanno's, and Hanno's scalp contracted under the pressure.

'The worm will come at the rising of the sun and at the rising of the moon it will return whence it came, and there shall be no mark on me.'

In the weak and innocent daylight he looked more than ever a creature of the dark. His hair hung longer than Hanno's about his sparsely bearded jaws, his hands and feet were gloved and slippered in grime and round his neck he wore, in place of the dead summer flowers, a skeletal wreath of brittle stems; bracken, kecksies, rushes and black bean husks.

'On that day, the sand will run and run. The man who bleeds in the face shall see it.' Aram turned and went back into the shadows.

'What does he mean?' said Dow. 'No mark on him?'

'He says that his head will be cloven like a cheese, and his spirit will be taken up through it and he will be found with no mark on him,' said Hanno.

'That's new,' said Cariola.

'Not to me,' said Hanno, bitterly.

'With no mark on him.' For once Dow seemed disinclined to mock. 'Dead?'

'I suppose so.'

'The man who bleeds in the face. I wonder what he means.'

'When does he ever mean anything?'

The Book said that no brazier might stand inside the sanctuary.

'Why? Because the smoke would defile the Holy Place, that's why,' said the acolyte, who took care to see that a brazier stood just outside the door of the Robing Room. The cookhouse glowed; the well of the temple filled with greasy fumes; even Aram equipped himself with a little perforated pot of charcoal and stewed gently in his fusty burrow. Only the sanctuary remained unheated, a plateau of ice, and under his inadequate blanket Hanno lay sleepless, night after night, shaking with cold.

'Why can't I have another blanket?'

'Because the Book says. . .'

The Book, the Book, the Book.

If he didn't die of boredom he would die of cold. In desperation he piled all his spare clothing on the couch and went foraging behind the altar for bedding. That quest yielded a sheepskin, stiff with old age, and a ragged quilt, incongruously embroidered with daisies. Since the Book proscribed it, he hid his plunder during the day and brought it out only after dark when he crawled into bed, fully dressed. He began to cough.

If he coughed at night, Aram materialized in the dark and spoke cheerfully of worms, which did nothing to ease the pain in his chest. When he coughed at mealtimes Dow recommended raw garlic and vinegar. Finally he began to cough during a service and couldn't stop. This time even the priest noticed and when he came out of the Robing Room one of the Guardians was waiting to take him to the priest's quarters. He went there, still coughing at intervals, and waited in the wide light room that overlooked the garden. A little snow had fallen and the lawn, that had been dappled with daisies, was now speckled with a different white. In the distance a gardener moved glumly to and fro, bent double and cutting cabbages.

Inside, a hot fire burned in a basket against the wall and thick curtains baffled the draught. On a ledge beside them a sand clock poured away the minutes but the priest did not come. Hanno stood and coughed and watched the clock spilling time in the silence, and thought of Aram. *And the sand shall run and run through the glass on that day.* Well, why not? Sand runs through glass every day. See it run.

The last of the sand trickled on to the summit of its little pyramid. An alert hand came between the curtains and turned the clock, and the sand started to fall once more. Hanno had the unsettling impression that time itself had been turned back and they were about to run through the same hour again. Still the priest did not come.

Hanno went over to the fire and knelt in front of it with more fervent adoration than he had ever demonstrated at the altar. The room gathered about him like a comforting shawl. He closed his eyes and dozed and nodded, until he realized that if he fell asleep with his head in the fire any concern for his future would be purely academic. Then he forced his eyes open and saw the hand come out from behind the curtain and turn the clock again. More than an hour had passed since he entered the room, and still no one came. The priest had forgotten him, just as his family had forgotten him. Was he really so forgettable? Anise? Ivo?

The curtains parted and the priest stepped through. He halted on the far side of the fire basket and stood there, looking down at Hanno, the lines of his face composed into an intricate diagram of compassion. Hanno understood that the old man thought he had passed out, and was chiding himself for his lack of observation.

And so he damned well should, Hanno said to himself. He wondered if his new-found acting ability would stretch to a convincing imitation of consumption, but the fear that he might actually have it restrained him. Without trying he began to cough again, rasping like a blunt saw on brick.

'You are ill,' said the priest, cleverly.

'I'm cold,' said Hanno. 'I am always cold.'

'They told me you had walked in the rain without sandals,' said the priest. 'That was foolish. Now you are ill.'

'I have no sandals.' Egil had forgotten to remember to give them back.

'You shall have your sandals. The surgeon must see you.'

'I'm cold.' He felt his face set rigid with obstinacy.

'You must not go out in the rain.'

'I'm cold.'

The priest, apparently under the impression that he was delirious, bent over him. 'You seem to be suffering. You are not required to suffer, only to serve.'

'I don't suffer. I'm cold. That's all. Cold.'

'How long have you been with us?'

'Four months – nearly five.' Don't I know every day, every hour?

'You should have a holiday,' said the priest. 'This afternoon you may go and visit your family.'

8

HIS cough forgotten he almost ran back to the Hut and very nearly sang. Only wait and you shall have your reward. See, Hanno, that's what comes of keeping your mouth shut: a willing Shepherd. He sat on the couch, still warm from his encounter with the fire and radiant with another warmth that was all his own. A moment later Dow appeared in the doorway and, seeing his pleasure, smiled a little in sympathy.

'I'm very happy for you.' He laid a heap of clothes on the couch. 'It's going to snow again. You'll need these.'

Hanno turned over the heap eagerly, like a child unwrapping a gift. He knew exactly how he must look, and didn't care. On to the couch fell his sandals, woollen footcloths and a pair of boots, similar to the ones that Dow wore as a Guardian.

'Egil's,' said Dow. 'We measured them against your sandals. His were the only ones that would fit.'

Hanno was not overjoyed at the prospect of wearing Egil's boots, but still he didn't care. The bundle was wrapped up with a long thick strip of cloth like a shepherd's plaid.

'It's a shepherd's plaid,' said Dow. 'We borrowed it from a shepherd.'

'The fellow who c-c-c-carried the lamb that day?'

'That's right. Be calm,' said Dow, laughing. 'You aren't going until after the midday meal.'

Hanno laughed too, shamefaced, and began to stow the garments under his table.

'You won't be able to stay long.'

'It doesn't matter.'

'I'll meet you on the steps, after we've eaten.'

'What?'

Dow looked faintly uncomfortable. 'I'm going with you.'

'I don't want. . .don't need. . .' Hanno dropped the sandals on the floor. 'Why?'

'The Shepherd never goes out alone.' Hanno watched him, his pleasure slipping away like sand. 'The Book says so.'

'Don't you trust me?'

'Of course we trust you. It's the Book.'

'Do you think I wouldn't come back? After all this time? I swear I would.'

'It doesn't matter what I think,' said Dow, backing away. 'It's the Book.'

The Book.

He walked over the frozen flowers, rose, mallow, lily, hemlock, clover, and sat down on the sanctuary steps to pull on his boots – Egil's boots. In the colonnade Dow waited for him, closely muffled in a white cloak. Hanno wound himself in the plaid, slung the loose end over his shoulder and went down to meet him.

'You aren't supposed to wear it like that,' said Dow, patiently.

'This way's warmest. Are you ashamed to be seen with me?' said Hanno. 'I don't mind at all if you'd rather not come.'

'Someone has to go with you.' Dow looked resigned, but resignation was one of his pleasures in life; resignation to being rained on; resignation to eating onions; resignation to accompanying Hanno's own louche person about the city. Why deny him his pleasures?

'I don't know why you don't tie a string round my neck and have done with it,' Hanno said.

'Don't be silly. It's the custom. The Shepherd never goes out alone.'

'In case he doesn't come back?'

'Look, it's part of the Ritual, that's all. We're here by choice, you aren't.'

'A willing Shepherd would come back,' said Hanno. 'Aren't I yet willing enough?'

'It's the Book...'

Hanno tweaked at Dow's girdle. 'Here, lead me along on the end of that and I'll go on all fours and bleat.' Dow frowned. 'You ought to keep me in a cage.'

'Be quiet.'

'And poke bread through the bars.'

'That's enough.'

'Or onions.'

They were passing through the wicket of the great gate. The guard locked it behind them.

'I didn't know you felt so badly about it.'

'Nor did I.'

The narrow lane that led to the temple was deserted. Hanno walked easily. The wind slashed at his wrists like an icy razor but the threatened snow had not fallen and the sky was blue between the high walls. A single gull slipped sideways and coasted on a current of air above him and he tilted his head to watch it, so that he ran straight into the first person who crossed his path. They cursed each other roundly and explicitly and Dow raised his eyebrows at hearing such language from the Shepherd.

He went in front after that, a volatile buffer between Hanno and the city. He was surprisingly light on his feet, dancing ahead with his elbows out, cleaving a path, dodging obstructions, leaving Hanno to follow him, more slowly, more heavily. Hanno felt like a cumbersome animal lumbering in his wake – on the end of a string.

The route was unfamiliar. 'This isn't the way to my

house,' he protested, searching hopelessly for a landmark among the sheds and hovels. 'I don't live here.'

'Ah, but I did,' said Dow. 'This is the way I came when I used to visit you. Remember those days?'

'I remember.' Dow turned along a downhill lane where water ran down the middle. An urbane pig came lounging past them in the opposite direction. The pig's owner hurried behind, less polished than his animal, and shouldered Hanno aside. Dow, you surely have gone up in the world. They turned another corner and verminous children scattered to let them by. Dow was well ahead now, and it was several seconds before he turned to see if Hanno were following him.

I could have lost him, then, thought Hanno, who was indeed following. I could have gone the other way. He guessed that it was fear of being absorbed into the roaring crowds that kept him tacked to Dow's heels. He remembered that he had always been afraid of crowds, to the extent of staying out of them, but had he always been *so* afraid? Dow halted under an archway and waited for him to catch up, impatient, anxious for the next move. I could catch him by the neck and crack it and drop him and run.

Run where?

'We're coming to the river,' said Dow.

'I know. I know where we are now. This alley leads to the Mill Bridge.' I wonder, is my boat there? I could get in it, cast off, get away before he –

'Come on.'

On the other hand, I could just walk away. What could he do about it? They must trust me to go back or they really would have had me on a string.

'There you are,' said Dow. They were standing at the head of the alley and before them lay the bridge and the river; and the house. Hanno leaned on the parapet of the bridge and looked downstream towards his home. The last time he had walked here he had been arguing with Ivo and it had passed from his sight before he ever looked back for a last glimpse.

Dow pointed to the steps. 'That's the way I used to come.'

'That's the way I come too. Why not?' He started down the steps.

'We're not really dressed for it.'

'Oh, come on; come on.' Hanno was smiling again. 'The grass is short in winter.' Without waiting to see if Dow would follow he jumped down the last half-dozen steps and strode along the bank, grinding down the stiff grass with Egil's boots. Dow *was* following him – very closely.

'The river's running high,' he said, drawing alongside.

Hanno felt that he didn't care to be so close to the river with Dow beside him. Who knew better than he did what a fast-running river could do? He has got me on a string and he knows it. He could have winked at all this. He could have turned his back and waited for me somewhere. He doesn't trust me. None of them does.

They came to the fence and Hanno stepped over it. Dow hesitated on the other side and put his hands on the top of the gate.

'Don't vault over it for god's sake,' said Hanno. 'It will collapse.'

'It won't open,' said Dow, looking at the knots of dead bindweed.

'How will you get in then?' Hanno asked, maliciously. In the boughs of the plum tree the gardener had hung up a dead crow, to encourage the others. Hanno swung it where it dangled by its feet, and considered chucking it at Dow. Then they could fight again, just as in the old days. He would love to take a good swing at Dow, for old time's sake, and for the sake of the last five months. He decided against it. Dow wouldn't fight; he would preach.

He had left something of his dignity behind, however. He

took a short run at the fence and straddled it, landing with a thud on the frozen earth.

At the back of the house the half-door stood open as ever. Hanno leaned over it and fumbled for the latch, calling as he always did, 'Hulloa?'

A voice answered him. 'What do you think you're doing?'

It was not a voice that he knew and he spun round, his fist already clenching.

'I saw you sneaking over the fence.' A man was standing behind him, with an iron bar in his hand. 'Who are you?'

'Who are you?' said Hanno. He was too bewildered to stand on his rights. Five months gone, and he was taken for a stranger at his own back door.

'You can tell me, first,' said the man. He put his head in at the door. 'Hey, Nan, bring the dog out. We've got trouble here.'

'A dog?' said Hanno. 'There's no dog.'

'Ho, but there is,' said the man. Inside the house a chain rattled, and a depraved-looking mastiff put its head and shoulders over the half-door. Its forefeet, like two cudgels, hung down in front. It did not bark; it sneered.

'What's that horrible thing doing here?' said Hanno. 'Who's Nan? Who are you?'

'That is indeed a horrible thing,' said the man. 'And if you was to come any closer I wouldn't vouch for your safety. Now, who are you?'

'Why don't you tell him?' said Dow. 'One of you has got to give in.'

Hanno was staring at the dog.

'Whaaaat?'

'It's a guard dog,' said the man. 'My dog, as it happens, and very unpredictable. When the young man left the old'un felt unsafe at nights, so they called us in, my pup and me. His name's Belabour.'

'They got that animal because I left? They got a dog instead of me?' said Hanno, incredulous. He didn't know whether to laugh or spit.

'You? You ain't Hanno?' said the dog handler. 'Here, Nan, come this ways a minute. There's a lad here, says he's Hanno.'

'Who's Nan?' The dog Belabour slid down from the door and made way for someone approaching from the other side. Hanno's old nurse appeared in the doorway.

'This here is Nan,' said Belabour's master. 'Now then, Nan, who's this?'

The old woman looked out, at first cautious, then astonished. Tremulously she folded her hands across her breast and said, 'It's the Shepherd.'

'No,' said Hanno. 'No, it's not; not here. It's only Hanno.'

'Well then, young sir, in that case I apologize,' said the dog handler. His unlovely companion pushed open the door and slouched out to join him. They began to move away, with some signs of contrition. 'But you shouldn't ought to have come round the back. Gentry and holiness goes to the front. We took you for a felon. Walk on, Belabour.'

'He's right. You should have come to the front door,' said Nurse, both reverent and reproving.

'Are you going to let me in?' said Hanno.

'And who is this person?'

'This is Dow.'

'We're old friends,' said Dow.

'Will you get out of the doorway,' said Hanno. 'I want to come in.'

'Is he coming in?'

Hanno turned questioningly to Dow, who was leaning against the pump, smirking.

'I'll wait outside,' said Dow.

'Aren't you afraid I'll sneak out the other way?' said

Hanno, already put out by his reception and chagrined that Dow should have witnessed it. The account of the Shepherd's homecoming should furnish an entertaining anecdote in the Guardians' hall tonight. 'There's more than one door, here.'

'You wouldn't do that,' said Dow, easily. 'Anyway, I don't want to disturb you. I can amuse myself.'

Hanno nodded, beyond caring one way or the other, and pushed past Nurse to get inside. She recovered some of her usual spirit.

'Your manners ain't improved any.'

He ignored her. She was showing off, the old bat, so that Dow should see that she was really unimpressed by Hanno's status. He wished he could believe it.

Inside the house nothing had changed, at first. The tiled floors glowed with warmth and cleanliness; resinous logs burned in every room. Hanno went down the hall to his father's study and threw open the door without knocking.

'Father?'

The man at the desk turned round. It was not his father.

'Who are you?' they both said, simultaneously.

The latest stranger stood up and came towards him.

'I am the master's secretary and you, whoever you are, should know better than to enter a private room without waiting to be admitted.'

'But I live here,' said Hanno, falling back in spite of himself, towards the door.

The secretary's face softened. 'Then you must be the younger son. Hanno, isn't it?'

'Yes.'

'The Shepherd.' He joined his fingers under his chin and bowed slightly.

'I wish you wouldn't do that,' said Hanno. 'I'm not the Shepherd here.'

'You are the Shepherd wherever you go,' said the secretary. 'Won't you stay? We could go into the parlour and I will send for some wine.'

Treated as an honoured guest in his own home, Hanno had little option but to follow him. 'How long have you been working here?'

'About three months. Ah, here we are. Will you sit? This is a very comfortable chair.'

'I know it is,' said Hanno. 'I made it.'

'You were a carpenter?'

'I could – can work with wood. I can do most things with my hands,' he said, cracking his knuckles reflectively.

'That can cause a rheum in the joints in old age,' the secretary remarked. 'Will you take wine?'

'Look, this is a delightful conversation, but', said Hanno, 'I came home to see my family. Where is it?'

'Your father has gone to a meeting of the chief burgesses, to debate the temple taxes,' said the secretary. 'I'm afraid I don't know when he will return. Your brother, of course, is rarely at home.'

'Is he at the pottery now?'

'I'm afraid I don't know where he is.'

'So you couldn't send a message to tell him I'm here.'

'I'm afraid not.'

'Oh my, you are a fearful man, aren't you,' said Hanno. A flutter of white caught his eye. The small panes of the window were hazed with moisture, but beyond them a figure moved to and fro in the garden. Dow's wind-whipped cloak caught all the brightness of the day and shone. Still on sentry duty.

'I'll wait,' said Hanno. 'I'll wait here.'

'I'm afraid I can't wait with you,' said the secretary. 'I have much work to do. But you may wait as long as you like.'

'I intend to.' The secretary left him sitting there. Hanno stretched out in his chair and tried to rid himself of the sensation that he was a visitor. He said, over and over again, I live here. I live here. I live here. After a while he got up and went into the kitchen. Nothing had changed, at first. The gardener and the footman were rolling dice at the table. The cook was kneading dough in the trough. Nurse was sewing.

'Hullo,' he said. They looked up at him, shyly, and made little nervous bobs with their heads. Then he saw Belabour, stretched out in front of the fire as though he owned it, wheezing like a hairy bagpipe. When he noticed Hanno he bared his teeth, suggesting that he could inflict terrible wounds if he felt like it, and fell asleep again. Hanno walked round him, suppressing an urge to kick, and went to stand beside Nurse.

'Why didn't you come and talk to me?' he said.

She looked sideways at him.

'In the parlour? That wouldn't be right.'

'You never bothered about that before.'

'It's different now.'

'I'm not different.'

'When you were here we all did as we liked.'

'But I shall come back again. I shall only be Shepherd until the next Festival.'

'Things won't be the same, even so.' She looked at him again. 'You are different.'

'It's the boots, maybe?' He smiled at her, encouragingly.

'No. I don't know...' She seemed puzzled. 'You don't look well.'

'That's a very cold temple. I tell you what,' he said, with a sudden burst of confidence, 'they're trying to freeze me to death.'

'Don't say things like that,' she said, scandalized. 'It's not proper. And you the Shepherd.'

'Do you ever come to the services?'

'Once in a while. I must say, you do it very nicely.'

'Oh, come now. I only stand.'

'Well, you stand nicely. You always did. You carry your height well. I saw to that,' she said, smugly. She was thawing. He leaned closer. 'Mind you, you were drooping about like a sick hen when I saw you in the garden.'

'You said yourself that I didn't look well.' He relaxed, consoled by the old familiar nagging.

'No need to lean on things like you're going to keel over any moment. Look at you now; your back's bent like a fish hook.' He straightened up. 'And I don't like your colour.'

'I've never had much colour.'

'You've got rings round your eyes. What do they feed you on?'

'Onions,' said Hanno. He looked out of the window. The restlessly patrolling figure had settled down on a stone urn and sat there shining like a salt lick in the sun. 'When will Father be home?'

'I don't know. Nobody tells me anything. Ask that secretary person.'

'He doesn't know either. Do you know where I could find Ivo?'

'I daresay he's at the pottery.'

'Why don't they come to the services?'

'You're a fine one to be asking that. When did you ever go?'

'They always did.'

'They still do. Your father, at any rate. Two or three times a week.'

'He doesn't!'

'Are you calling me a liar?'

'I thought, if he came, he would ask to see me.'

'Perhaps it's not allowed.'

'Perhaps it isn't.' It probably wasn't. He didn't know whether to be hurt because his father had not tried to see him, or glad that he bothered to come to the services. But then, he had always come. If he still came, it wasn't on his son's account.

'What about Ivo?'

'How should I know what Ivo does? He's hardly ever here.'

A strident bell rang through the house. Belabour lifted his head and growled. The footman scooped up his dice and rose from the table.

'The old man's back,' he said. 'Begging your pardon,' he added, apologetically, to Hanno. 'I'll tell him you're here.'

'No. No, don't. I'll come with you.'

The footman looked embarrassed and mumbled, 'It's not proper. You should have waited in the parlour.'

'Don't be a fool, man. I never used to go into the parlour, did I?'

'It's different now.'

They wrangled down the length of the corridor and only stopped when they came out into the hall. Hanno paused in the mouth of the entry and waited for his father to see him. He was involved in taking off his hood and cloak and it was some seconds before he noticed who was there. He blinked in amazement. Hanno held out his arms.

'Father?'

He waited for the certain embrace that should follow, but his father only stood there.

'Why are you here?'

'I came to see you,' said Hanno. 'They said I might come to see you.' The last shreds of his happiness fell from him. 'Don't you want to see me?'

His father moved at last, came forward with his arms outstretched, but the old man advanced with constraint and the hands that should have held Hanno and hugged him only rested on his shoulders.

'My son.'

Hanno tried to lift his mouth into a smile, but all the curl had gone out of it.

'Are you well, my son?'

It was like a rehearsal of his interview with the priest. He said, automatically, 'I'm cold.'

The footman went past them with a second cloak. Hanno noticed that his father had not come home alone. An elderly man was standing by the door, dressed like a dignitary. Hanno did not recognize him, but he recognized authority. This was one of his father's friends who had been kept out of his way in the days of the boat. His father beckoned the visitor forward.

'This is my son,' he said, with pride. 'The Shepherd.'

'I'm Hanno,' said Hanno, and held out his hand. His only reply was a stiff bow, such as a proud man would give, reluctantly, to his superior. He let his hand drop.

'Are you going to stay and eat with us?' said his father.

'I'm afraid not,' said a voice behind them, in the passage. The words were the secretary's but the voice was Dow's. 'It's time to go.'

Hanno twisted round. 'But I've only just come.'

'Not quite,' said Dow.

'Half an hour ago.'

'It's time.'

'My son, if the temple calls you, you must go,' said his father, sounding almost relieved, as if the strain of having the Shepherd in the house might prove too much for his heart.

'There's no need. We needn't go yet.'

'We have to be back in time for the Evening Service,' said Dow. 'Next time he can come a little earlier, perhaps.'

'Goodbye, my son,' said his father. Hanno felt that a shutter was closing firmly in his face.

'Tell Ivo I came.'

'Of course.'

'Tell him to come and see me.'

'Of course. Now you must go; see, the young man is waiting.'

'Let him wait.' Dow had the door open already, took him by the arm and began to draw him towards the step. 'Let go my arm.'

'It's time.'

'Father – tell Ivo – ask him, please –'

'Goodbye, my son.'

The door closed between them.

'We'll go back by the road,' said Dow, guiding him firmly round the corner of the house. Belabour saw them off the premises, panting and grinning at the gate.

On the road Dow released his hold and Hanno strode ahead in a frenzy of humiliation and disappointment. Dow did not break his silence or try to catch up with him, but walked very close behind. As they came out on to the bridge, by the steps, Hanno stopped and turned on him.

'You had no right. No right.'

'I did,' Dow said, quietly. 'I have to see that you return in time.'

'In time? If we walked backwards with our eyes shut we'd be in time.' He crowded Dow towards the head of the steps. 'I could kick you into the river from here.'

'No,' said Dow. 'Don't do that.' It sounded more like a warning than a request. Hanno turned from him and started across the bridge, Dow at his heels.

'Don't walk so close.' Heel and toe. Heel and toe. 'We'll go back my way. I don't care for your quarter.' Like a shadow. 'You're afraid to let me out of your sight.'

They entered an echoing chasm between two warehouses.

'Your father understood,' said Dow.

'He thought we were friends.'

'Are we not?'

'Walk beside me, Friend, or in front. I don't like being followed.'

'There's no room here to walk two abreast.'

'In front then, as we did coming.' Hanno stood back against the wall of the alley to let him overtake. Dow stood still. 'Go on. In front.'

'Wait till we get out of the alley.'

'Get in front, I said. I don't like you breathing down my neck.' Dow stayed where he was. 'Move, damn you.'

'There's no room.'

'There's room to pass, look, plenty of room. I'm not moving on until you get in front. You didn't care that I went behind on the way out.'

'That was different.'

'Everything's different,' said Hanno, his voice rising. 'You're not the only one who's noticed. You don't trust me to come back, do you? You think I'll cut and run. Well, I don't care if we stay here all day; it's you that's in a hurry to get back, not me. See, I'll sit. I'm in no hurry to go. I'll sit.'

He sat.

Dow was pitifully anxious to behave as though nothing had happened. 'I'm sorry. I didn't know the visit had upset you so much. Perhaps it would be better if you didn't go again.'

'I'll go again when I want to go again. And I won't be going with you.'

'Shepherd, be sensible. You can't sit here all day.'

'Can't I? What are you going to do about it, go back and fetch the dog? Walk on, Belabour? Walk on, Hanno? Good dog. Good sheep!'

Dow crouched beside him. 'I have to take you back. Be sensible.'

'Are you going to carry me?' Hanno looked at Dow's lesser figure and began to laugh joylessly at the idea. 'You and the dog both?'

'That's better. Now, get up, do. Please.'

'All right.' Lacking the energy to prolong his outburst he stood up. He stood up too quickly, and the waiting pain split his face like a cleaver. 'I was supposed to feel better after this,' he said, resentfully, his hand over his eyes and groping along the wall like a blind man.

'Your cough's better,' said Dow, unhelpfully. They moved on. They were almost out of the alley before he could look up and notice that Dow was still walking behind him.

They passed through the market, elbowed and jostled but never parted for an instant. Without turning his head Hanno could see the white cloak shining at his back. He muttered as he walked, 'I don't like you, Dow. I never have liked you and now I like you less than ever. You have me on a string.' On the way out the string had been slack; now it was tightening. Hanno felt the constriction about his throat.

There was a small uproar immediately behind him. Hanno looked round and saw that a cart had overturned on the icy setts. A landslide of mangolds was blocking the street and Dow was on the other side of it. As he watched, the cart tilted further, shedding another avalanche of roots. Hanno had no thought of running until he saw Dow's apprehensive eyes glance up at him. He dived sideways into the crowd.

No one made way for him, but neither did anyone obstruct him. The market place was all on the move, surging purposelessly. He shoved, and was shoved; stumbled, looking over his shoulder at every step, but wherever he went the crowd closed behind him like cornstalks. Even now, Dow might be buried under the mangolds; at all events, he was out of sight. Hanno gave up trying to run and floundered to a halt against the nearest wall.

It came to him as he stood there, trying to regain his breath, that he had acted with quite extraordinary foolishness. What could he do now? He had fled on impulse, because of the string round his neck; but there was no string round his neck. Why was he breathless? He had hurried, and it had been no more than hurrying, less than a hundred yards, and yet already he was almost too exhausted to stand upright. Once he could have run for three or four miles at an easy lope, and enjoyed it. What could he do now? Either he went back to the temple or he did not. If he did not, where could he go? Certainly not home again. He could not stay where he was any longer. The Book might maintain that when people saw him in his head-dress they saw only the Shepherd; all the same, quite a lot of those people knew who *he* was: Hanno the Shepherd, unknown but famous. Several people were looking at him now. He sent his imagination among them and looked back, momentarily dismayed by the curious sight he must present. Dow was out there somewhere. He had only to say, Have you seen the shepherd? to half a dozen people, before someone answered: Over there, having a fit by Potter's Street.

He slid backwards into the nearest doorway. Almost every building on that street housed a pottery, but Ivo's, thank god, was at the other end. An hour ago Hanno would have run straight to him, certain of help and comfort. Now he was less certain. In his early days at the pottery Ivo had spent many hours in the temple, studying the designs which, eventually, he would have the responsibility of reproducing. He had come home talking wondrously of temple customs. He knew the rituals as well as Hanno did, probably better. He would undoubtedly have something to say at the sight of his brother the Shepherd, on the loose and without an escort.

Hanno had chosen the wrong refuge. Most of the potteries kept their kilns in a separate outbuilding at the back, but this was an ancient business, unmodernized. A kiln was roaring at his side. Two youths, sufficiently alike in their clayey garments to be twins, were ministering to it. One fed logs into the furnace beneath: the other operated bellows. They looked at each other, at Hanno, at each other, and exchanged a single remark. So close to the kiln it was impossible to hear what was said, but Hanno saw their lips part in a concerted Sssssh...

Ssssshepherd.

He was as well trapped outside the temple as he was inside. He smiled at the two apprentices; a sheep's smile, without any thought in it, and started to go out as he had come in, backwards. As he reached the doorway something gripped his right arm from behind and twisted it sharply. The building cartwheeled away from him, the street slewed over his head, and he found himself kneeling in the gutter, his face against the kerbstone and a hand, that emerged from a blindingly white sleeve, biting into his shoulder. Another hand, which he could not see, held his arm wrenched up against his back.

'Now, what did you go and do that for?' said Dow, in the injured tone of a nursemaid left in charge of a wayward child.

'Let me get up.' From his severely limited viewpoint he could see feet gathering, their owners attracted by Dow's strenuous sleight of hand.

'You won't try to run?'

'How can I?'

The hand disappeared from his shoulder. The pressure on his arm was relaxed but not removed. By Dow's good grace he rose to his feet, aware that without Dow's good grace he would be down on his face again if he made an ill-considered move. He looked at the ground, rather than look at the people who were looking at him. In the pottery two identical pairs of feet, spattered with clay, stood side by side. Snow was falling. He began to cough.

9

Dow behaved as though none of this had taken place.

When he greeted Hanno next morning he was no less courteous than usual, and no more. He smiled, nodded, and would have passed on, but Hanno stepped in front of him, barring his way.

'Wait.'

Dow stopped, still courteous, his very courtesy implying that they both knew why he had stopped. He had stopped because he had no objection to hearing whatever it was that Hanno wanted to say. If he chose to walk past, there was nothing Hanno could do about it. Hanno had been foolish enough to believe that his superior height and strength gave him the advantage. Hanno's right arm hung useless at his side, to remind him of his mistake.

'I wasn't trying to escape from you, yesterday.'

'I know. Of course you weren't.'

'I wanted to come back alone.' Not on a string.

'I understand.'

'Not followed.'

'Yes. I understand.'

'Then why did you follow me?'

'Because the Book says that the Shepherd must be attended at all times.' He was still smiling. Hanno tried to return his smile.

'I thought you were going to take my arm off.'

'I didn't break it.'

'No.'

'I took care not to.' In other words, I could have done. 'It was only a precaution.'

'It was very clever. How did you do it?'

'It's one of the Old Arts, handed down from one generation to another; from Guardian to Guardian.' In other words, Shepherd, you aren't going to learn how it's done. 'It is called The Knowledge that Makes a Small Man Great. You understand that, don't you?'

'Yes. I understand that.'

'Or, that makes a tall man humble.' He laughed merrily, as if they were sharing a joke. 'Do you remember, when we were children, how we used to fight for fun? You always won, didn't you, when we fought face to face. Well, not all battles are fought face to face.'

'Could you by any chance be using your old art to settle an old grudge?' said Hanno, unguardedly. Dow's smile became warped at the corners, and his arm came up, oddly crooked at the elbow. Hanno fell back a pace or two.

'The Shepherd cannot go where he likes. Nor can he say what he likes,' said Dow, with no vestige of courtesy. 'That was sacrilege. Remember what a fool I can make of you. Think what a dozen of us could do.'

Hanno watched him walk across the pavement towards the gate, through which he might come and go as he pleased; a small man made great by knowledge. Hanno had no knowledge. The Shepherd was not required to know anything.

Cariola was coming towards him. Hurriedly he tucked his poor arm into the front of his tunic before she should notice the swelling, ask him what was wrong and set about him in an effort to make him better. But Cariola knew; she shook her head sadly and patted him consolingly on his damaged shoulder. It felt like being walloped with an oar. Hanno winced against a column. For all he knew, Cariola too might be in possession of a secret that enabled her to throw him halfway across the temple with the flick of a finger.

'It's time for the service,' she said. 'Oughtn't you to be dressing? Will you need any help?'

'No.' Oh, god, no. She would probably detach his arm altogether, in an excess of pity.

He started to cross the sanctuary, towards the gate in the railing, but before he got to it, there was Aram, coming crab-wise from behind the altar, smiting the air with his bundle of reeds; murmuring hollowly like a conduit. He took Hanno by the sleeve. Hands; everywhere hands; such little hands, and his own so large and so useless.

'Are you prepared for the day of the worm?' Aram demanded.

'I'm not prepared for anything,' Hanno said, sulkily.

'On that day I shall be taken up, and there shall be no mark on me.'

'May that day be soon,' said Hanno, adopting Aram's tone of formal lunacy. He looked Aram in the eye. It was as rewarding as looking into a dark hole. 'Aram, how many Shepherds have you known?'

'All Shepherds are as one to me,' said Aram.

'Do you know my name?'

'You have no name. You are the Shepherd.'

'My name is Hanno.'

'The world is in a wheel,' said Aram. 'The world turns and the wheel turns not.' He brandished his swatch of reeds and moved off.

'My name is Hanno.'

Aram looked back. 'I shall be found with no mark on me. What will become of you?'

'What will become of me?' His voice tore, shockingly. 'Aram! *What will become of me?*'

Anyone else would have turned in alarm. Aram continued in his horrid gait across the sanctuary, the reeds describing strange symbols in the air above his head.

*

Dow went on behaving as though nothing had happened. He was still off-duty when the service ended, and when Hanno came out of the Robing Room he tucked an affable arm through Hanno's arm and walked with him, steered him, in the direction of the fountain.

'I saw your father at the Service,' he said.

'Did you?' What's it to me, that you saw him?

'He asked if you were well.'

'And am I?'

'I told him you were very well,' said Dow, and gave his arm an agonizing squeeze.

Four or five other Guardians were at the fountain before them, among them Egil and one Frey, Dow's cousin; a smaller Dow, but equally boring. Muffled in their white cloaks they had brushed the light snow from the fountain's rim, and rested there in attitudes of alert severity, looking to Hanno like members of a tribunal assembled in emergency. He looked from one to another. Why are they here? Why am I here?

What am I for?

Nearby sat Cariola and Nola, a cottage loaf and a cake. Having no flowers to entwine, they wove garlands of evergreen, cedar and ivy, with red briony berries like eyes among the leaves. Dow sat on the edge of the basin and Hanno was pulled down beside him. Cariola dropped her garland to skim flat pebbles across the frozen surface, and the water slapped threateningly where the ice shattered. Hanno tried to turn a little, so that he could at least see his enemy, but Dow tightened his friendly grip. Now he knew that Hanno knew, he could hardly be expected to resist flexing his muscles.

'What was Aram saying to you today?'

'Only what he always says. Worms, mainly.'

'Worms?'

'He was speaking of the day of the worm. The Day of

the Worm,' he repeated, translating for Dow's benefit. 'When that day comes, he says, he will be found dead with no mark on him. You've heard him yourself.'

'I forget,' said Dow. 'How will he be found?'

'His head will be cloven like a cheese, and then the cleft will close.'

'Don't you believe him?' said Egil.

'Do you? If your head was cloven open like a cheese, wouldn't you expect it to leave a mark?'

'How do you think he will die, then?'

'I suppose he will just die, like anyone else,' said Hanno, annoyed by their interest. Once he would have shaken them off and they would have let him go, gibing good-naturedly at his want of sociability. That would never happen again. Cariola's arm lay across his shoulders like a rafter. 'Why should there be a mark on him? The city isn't at war. No one in the temple would harm him. Most people die without a mark on them.'

'Not at his age,' said Dow. 'He can't be much older than you.'

'I would have thought much older,' said Hanno. It did not seem to him that Aram's was a young man's madness.

'What else did he say?'

'He says the world is in a wheel. He thinks the world turns.' Why should anyone care what Aram thought? Usually they were only too grateful that he had attached himself to the Shepherd, thereby leaving the rest of them in peace. He did not want to talk about Aram. 'Does that mean something?' he demanded, truculently.

'It would be funny if it did, wouldn't it?' said Nola.

'It would not be Funny,' said Dow-the-governess. 'We are too ready to laugh at Things we don't Understand.'

'Don't look at me,' said Hanno. 'I've never laughed at him.'

'No, you haven't,' Egil said, thoughtfully. 'What *do* you think of him?'

'I think he's crazy,' said Hanno. 'When has anyone ever thought otherwise?'

'In the old days,' said Dow, 'many Holy Men were thought to be fools, before their deaths. And the greatest Miracle Worker of them all was said to be a madman.'

Hanno had been brought up on tales of the greatest miracle worker of them all, and, unmoved by Ivo's persuasive story-telling, was still of the opinion that he was a madman, but the water was at his back, and Dow was at his side.

'You think Aram may turn out to be a miracle worker?' he said, carefully. 'He certainly thinks so. It would be nice if he were right – nice for him, I mean.'

'It's a good thing someone understands him,' said Egil.

'I don't understand him.'

'But you feel for him?'

'Oh yes.' Poor sod. 'I wish he could die as he thinks he will.' He wished nothing of the kind, but he sensed that this was a day for doing what was expected of him.

Egil and Frey were staring at him like contemplatives trying to send themselves into a trance: he decided that whatever was expected, he had done enough. Dow's attention had wandered. Hanno stood up, suddenly, and moved away. Either Dow must let him go or be prepared to hurl himself at him. Watching Dow, he failed to notice that Frey and Egil had closed up. They leaned on him. The two girls smiled and smiled. They were his Friends, anxious to remind him of the fact. Dow looked at Egil, shook his head at Frey. They withdrew, also smiling, and let Hanno pass between them.

'Where are you going?' Dow asked, in his most natural manner.

'Nowhere.' Hanno only half-turned to answer him and did not stop.

'Then why not stay?'

'*No!*'

'It's all right,' said Dow. 'I'm not coming after you.'

Hanno looked round again and they were all watching him; all smiling.

Cariola waved.

He was no more alone.

Wherever he went his Friends went with him. They sat on his couch and chatted, shared his meals, escorted him to doors and met him when he came out of them.

'I only have to be accompanied when I go outside the gate,' said Hanno, turning savage one morning when he walked out of the Robing Room and found a small crowd awaiting him.

'But we're your Friends,' they protested, and Egil's fingers closed round his arm, to prove it.

The arm was a long while out of action. Hanno discovered the existence of the temple surgeon who stirred himself to squint into Hanno's open mouth like a ferret sizing up a rabbit hole, before giving him linctus for his cough and liniment for his arm. Neither had any effect, but one night, fumbling in the dark, he swallowed the liniment by mistake. He spent the hours until dawn in acute discomfort, waiting to die, until he realized that the cough had disappeared. The arm healed in its own time.

As soon as he recovered the use of his hand, he wrote a neatly phrased note to the priest, requesting permission to visit Ivo. In fact, he was no longer certain that he wanted to see Ivo while he was Shepherd, but he wanted to see what would happen. As he expected, his request was turned down.

'I think it would not be wise,' said the priest, 'so soon after your last time out. Dow says the cold air did you no good.'

'Is that what he says?' It was the cold air, was it?

'He says you came home very much disabled.' Clearly, Dow had not described to the priest exactly how they had come home.

'My cough is better.'

'Then we must not risk making it worse again. Be patient, my son. In less than seven months it will be the Festival again, and your time will be over.'

'I'm still cold.'

'The dark of the year is come and gone,' said the priest. 'All that can happen next is Spring.'

Shall I live so long?

The cold grew more and more intense and Hanno spent less and less time in the Hut, more time in the vicinity of the acolyte's brazier outside the Robing Room. He did not want for company; by now no one was able to keep warm, and the temple was filled with little conspiratorial groups that gathered round the glowing baskets. He removed a small earthenware bowl from the cookhouse, knocked a hole in it, borrowed some charcoal from a brazier and kept it with him at night. Nobody remarked on this, but one morning he discovered the bowl missing, and in its place an onion. He left it like a votive offering in Aram's den, averting his eyes from the tapestry, and the next time Aram came reeking upon him he was able to assume that the maniac had been subduing the spirit.

Aram was bearing aloft his favourite altar vessel, the one with the long neck.

'It shall be filled with blood,' he announced, and tilted it as if pouring a libation. 'See?'

Hanno thought briefly of the tapestry. 'If you say so.'

'Whose blood shall fill it, Shepherd?'

'Yours?' Hanno suggested, nastily. Aram was taken aback. He lowered the vase and retreated, treading tile by tile, as Hanno did. It was the first time, so far as Hanno could recall, that Aram had been visibly affected by anything that was said to him.

'I shall not bleed,' he muttered. 'There shall be no mark on me.'

Hanno felt that he had trespassed on Aram's most treasured illusion. He would have apologized, but he doubted if any apology would penetrate deep enough to take effect. He put out a conciliatory hand, but Aram darted out of reach, heading for the safety of his domain behind the altar, leaving Hanno to discover how it felt to have someone recoil from *him*.

He walked through the colonnade, past Dow, safely immobilized by duty, and went down the steps to the courtyard. Reluctantly he was drawn towards the gate. He stood a little way from it, surveying the massive hinges and more massive bolts: the latch, longer than his arm, the iron studs as large as his fist; surveyed in his turn by the guards who stood one each side of it.

'Not today, Shepherd,' said one. 'Not until the Festival.'

'I wouldn't try to bribe you,' Hanno said, 'and I have no money anyway, but if I did bribe you, would you let me go?'

'But? If? Would?' said the other guard. 'No.'

'We wouldn't,' said his companion, 'but others might. Others might take your money and then send your Friends after you. You'd be brought back, as you were last time.'

Hanno recalled how he had been brought back, last time, with bruised and bloody face, one arm locked behind his back; and followed by a curious crowd.

'Has it ever happened before?'

'I don't think it has,' said the guard. 'Not in our time, at any rate. Most Shepherds are only too happy to be in here. It's a peaceful kind of life compared with what goes on outside.'

'Life *is* outside,' said Hanno. 'I wasn't running away. I was coming back, only I wanted to come back alone.'

'No, never alone,' said the first guard. 'The Book says, so they tell us, The Shepherd may not go abroad alone.'

'This Shepherd may not go anywhere alone,' said Hanno. He saw Nola and Cariola, one tripping, one pounding, across the courtyard. 'Why not alone?'

The guard looked at him and produced the stock reply. 'Because the Shepherd is unwilling.'

'But the Shepherd becomes willing.'

'Never that willing.'

And then, one morning, he was alone.

Waiting for the noon service he lay on his couch and yawned and stretched and yawned. It was not a warm day but the dead weight of winter was lifting. For the first time that year Cariola had brought flowers to the service, hyacinths grown in the sheltered garden, and the scent of their growing still drifted through the temple. Breathing no longer hurt. He turned his face to the hurdles and closed his eyes, knowing that he could lie at last on a dry blanket, and without shivering. This was the cue for someone to bounce in and sit on his feet; shake him, rouse him, summon him to conversation or exercise. At any moment he would be hauled out of the Hut and exposed to Friendship. He breathed shallowly, stiff with expectation, awaiting the relentless smile and the prehensile hand on his shoulder.

No one came.

He rolled off the couch and looked out of the doorway. He saw no living thing, unless he was prepared to count the Guardians as living things. Spring had not touched them yet; they were frozen in their places. Faint sounds reached him from behind the doors of various halls; somewhere a bird celebrated with a few experimental notes, but the only movement he saw was at the altar, where one shadow approached another and absorbed it.

Aram.

He supposed that the Friends were all outside in the garden, trying to convince themselves that spring had arrived, and it appeared that they felt able to convince themselves without his assistance. He walked out into the sanctuary feeling half-relieved, half-neglected, unable to credit that he was truly alone for the first time in months. It was with a perverse sense of isolation that he looked towards the altar and was comforted by the sight of Aram prowling round it, selecting a vessel to receive his attentions. He padded up and down on his dirty feet, his hands swooping and hovering over the fleeces on the altar. After much hesitation he decided upon a certain bowl: out came the remnant of the god's garment and he went back into the dark carrying his burden on one arm, eyes downcast, looking for reflections in it, perhaps.

May you see what you want to see, thought Hanno, and turned to go down the steps to the well and from there to the courtyard. As he reached the sanctuary gate he saw Cariola coming the other way and instinctively he began to go back, pausing by a column as she hurried up the steps, to see which way she would turn. At the same moment Frey appeared in the well, and then the door of the slype opened and Egil came out. Nola was hurrying down the corridor from the priest's quarters. Hanno glanced from one to the other in bewilderment; had they all converged by accident or had they come looking for him? He no longer felt neglected. The prospect of the whole gang coming down on him at once was too much. He retreated in the only direction left open to him, the route to the altar, hemlock, lily, mallow, rose. They were coming after him and he felt like a deer driven by dogs towards a snare. Cariola was steaming up the steps, Frey leaning over the sanctuary rail. Dow suddenly joined Egil at the door of the slype. Any moment now and Aram would spring out underfoot, with a doom-laden shriek: *Shepherd!*

In the dim wastes behind the altar his foot struck something that yielded and then did not yield, so that he staggered and fell painfully on his hands, his foot entangled with whatever it was that had tripped him. He waited for the rush of feet and the battery of hands that would help him up, dust him down, shake and steady him; for Aram's eldritch eruption from his den. He looked up. He was still alone. He looked round. He had fallen over Aram.

Aram was sitting with his back against the back of the altar; in his lap the shallow bowl, and in his hand the remnant of the god's garment. His head drooped on his chest; the arm about the bowl was slack; the fingers that held the remnant were relaxed.

'Aram. I'm sorry – I'm so sorry. Did I hurt you?' He thought it unlikely that Aram would notice even if he were hurt, and he half-expected to be answered with an irrelevant prophecy concerning worms or wheels. Aram did not look up; Hanno knelt beside him and lifted his head. Aram's eyes were open.

'Aram, I'm sorry. Where are you hurt? Aram, answer me.' Say something, even if only to tell me that you'll be found dead without a mark – '*Aram!*'

At last someone arrived: Dow.

'What's the matter?' said Dow.

'He's dead,' said Hanno.

'So he is.'

'Did I do it?'

'Frey, Egil, come here, quick.'

'Did I do it?'

'Nola, what are you doing? Come here.' He sounded as though he were calling them to a celebration.

'Did I do it?'

'No, of course you didn't do it,' Dow snapped.

'You fell over his foot, that's all. I saw you fall,' said Cariola.

Hanno thought that no one had understood him.

'He's dead.'

'I can see that.' Dow's face was scarlet with an emotion that did not seem to be grief. 'He's dead, and you didn't do it.'

'He might have hit his head when I fell.'

'You didn't do it.' Hanno wished he felt as sure of that as Dow did.

Finally someone noticed his distress; Cariola, of course. She spread out at his side and put her arms round him.

'It's all right,' she said.

'But he's dead.' It seemed to him an appalling thing that anyone should die, sitting up, in the midst of life. Death should be a slow uncoiling of the spring, and Aram's spring had suddenly snapped.

'What's the matter with you?' said Egil. 'You didn't do it.'

'Are you sure?'

'Of course I'm sure.' Egil brought his face close to Hanno's and shouted. 'How can I not be sure? Look at him. He's dead and there's no mark on him!'

Hanno said, 'How can you be sure there's no mark on him?'

No one heard him. The priest was summoned and came running, slowly, borne forwards by the acolyte. All the Guardians were there; those on duty had left their posts and nobody rebuked them. The temple surgeon was summoned, and came, and sent for a colleague who lived in the city, not far from the gate. When the gate was opened those few worshippers who were waiting outside for the noon service ran to see what was happening. The news passed back and back into the city. Hanno was pushed ever further away from the centre of the *mêlée* but, somehow, never managed to reach the fringe of it. No matter where he was pushed or jostled a hand always fastened about his arm and drew him back into the crowd. He hardly knew what was happening any longer; the temple was filled with riot. He heard the Shepherd called for, once, and then again, and again as others took up the cry. The hand on his arm became many hands, and he was pulled back towards the altar, where the priest and the surgeons stood. Another voice screamed for silence; everyone screamed for silence, but eventually some screamers began to listen to others, and there was silence. Hanno understood that the silence was for him. They wanted to hear him speak. He would not speak.

The priest placed his gentle hands on Hanno's shoulders and said, 'You, my son? You found him?'

Hanno nodded.

'Say it aloud, my son. You found him?'

'I fell over him.'

'No.'

'Yes.' He turned his head, but it was impossible to see who had interrupted. 'I fell over his foot. I thought I'd –'

'No. You didn't touch him. You fell over this.' The speaker was Egil. He held up Aram's basket, squashed out of shape.

'I fell over his foot.'

'I was behind you. You fell over the basket. There was a rag covering it; perhaps that looked like a leg – to you.'

How can a wicker basket look like a leg? 'I thought I fell...'

'You fell over the basket!' Egil stepped up close and brandished the crumpled rag under Hanno's nose, as if he would stuff it into his mouth and silence his protests. Hanno perceived that he was not saying the right things. Perhaps he had fallen over the basket. He was no longer sure of anything.

'You never touched him.'

'Is that right, my son? You did not touch him?'

'I suppose not.'

'Say it aloud, my son. They want to hear you.'

'I didn't touch him.'

'And he was dead, as you see him now?'

Hanno looked down, not wanting to.

'Yes. That is...' Surely his mouth had been open: and his eyes.

'As you see him now?'

'Yes, but –'

'With no mark on him?'

'I don't know. I didn't...'

'The surgeons say there is no mark on him.'

'But I didn't see...' *I couldn't see.* Don't you know that? No, you don't, do you?

The priest turned to the crowd and lifted his hands. 'The prophecy is fulfilled.'

Prophecy? 'But he was mad.' His protest tailed off again as he looked at Aram. Dead, Aram looked no madder than anybody else; certainly no madder than Egil and considerably less mad than the priest. He wondered how he himself looked: red-eyed and stammering woefully about things that might never have happened.

'Tell it to the people,' cried the priest, in a new, firm voice, and the crowd disintegrated, turned and ran towards the gate and into the city; to tell the people that the prophecy was fulfilled.

'We have missed the noon service,' Hanno said to the priest. 'See, the sand clock has run out.'

'You can see the sand clock?' said Dow, strangely.

'It stands in the sunshine,' said Hanno, and thought he felt the snare again.

'Well, if we have missed the Service, the god will forgive us,' said the priest. 'These are strange times.'

Are they not? thought Hanno, as the old man moved away with his attendants and the surgeons busied themselves about the corpse, to prepare it for the eyes of the curious. The Guardians returned to their posts and the Friends sat about the fountain under the now cloudless sky, talking earnestly. He looked longingly towards the gate, but it was once more locked, and the guards stood to attention beside it. Something unnatural was happening to the gate. It bellied in and out like a sail in the wind, and boomed as it swelled and subsided.

The booming hurt his head, cruel booming gate. He looked down. A drop of blood fell on to his hand and he went away quickly, before anyone should see.

10

On the day after his death they took Aram and buried him, without any fuss, in the little funerary plot behind the temple garden. This interment was an elevation indeed. The plot was very small and only the upper echelons of those who Dwelt in the Temple could be sure of a place in it. Lesser persons were taken out to the pasture, and the sheep walked over their unmarked graves, but poor mad Aram, citizen of nowhere, was laid among priests. Hanno, who thought that he had known Aram better than anyone, asked to attend the funeral, but the priest refused.

'Would you distress yourself again?' he asked, when Hanno made it known that he wanted to follow the coffin, so Hanno sat in his Hut, looking out through the low doorway. Under the arch of the colonnade he saw the sun rise above the wall, swelling like a dusky blister until it pulled away and rose free into the shining sky. It was a lovely day for a funeral.

After the last footfalls had died away and a particular door had slammed for the last time, Cariola billowed into the Hut and settled beside him on the couch. She hugged herself with delicious daring, because as a Handmaiden she should not be alone and secluded with the Shepherd; not with any man, but the chaperone had gone to the burying ground, and those Guardians who were on duty had their backs to the Hut.

'I thought you would have gone to see him off,' said Hanno, uncomfortably aware of her disobedience and her glee.

'It would have been too sad,' said Cariola, sniffing experimentally, to see how sad she felt.

'You should be sad at a burying, surely,' said Hanno. 'No one thinks worse of you for showing it.'

'The priest said that too much grief would be out of place, under the circumstances. These are strange times, he said.' She touched an eyelid. There were no tears, so she gave up trying to hold down the corners of her mouth and smiled expansively, as if unlaced from a tight corset. 'I should have cried. I expect that's why he wouldn't let you go.'

'I don't think I should have cried,' said Hanno.

'You nearly did yesterday.' Her smile became tender at the memory. He guessed sourly that she hoped he would do it again, in the same spirit of man-eating charity with which she looked at his nose and hoped it would bleed. She enjoyed seeing him incapacitated. It occurred to him, in passing, that she almost certainly lacked Dow's knowledge of unarmed combat, or she would long ago have knocked him flat, and followed that up in a manner which defied his powers of imagination.

'Yesterday I was upset,' he said, and exposed all his teeth in a wild grin, to show how little upset he was now.

'It's strange how it all happened just as he said it would,' said Cariola.

'What happened? He said he would die, and he died. So shall I. So will you.'

'Without a mark on him.'

'So?'

'It was very sudden. We all saw him at the Morning Service, walking about. Didn't you?'

'I saw him a few minutes before I fell over him. Walking about.'

'You didn't fall over him,' said Cariola. 'You fell over his basket.'

'But you said, yourself, that you saw me fall over his foot.'

'No, I didn't, I didn't.'

'You said it.'

'I didn't see it. I was mistaken. You tripped on the basket.'

'All right. All right. I don't see that it matters whether I fell over his feet or his basket, so long as I didn't cause his death. You can't blame me for wondering. Think how you'd feel.'

'Oh no. No. It wasn't your fault. Everyone knows that.' She sat quietly for a little while, recovering her few wits. 'You never touched him.' Emotion worked in her like leaven in dough.

'So, there's no mark on him. Does that make him a prophet?' said Hanno.

'But he said it would happen.'

'He also said that the sky would open like the mouth of the basilisk. Did you see that, by any chance? Were there basilisks about, yesterday?'

'It rained.'

'Goodness me,' said Hanno, with heavy irony. 'That must have been the first time in all of two days.'

'It rained hard. The sky opened – that was what he meant. He used to say the most wonderful things.'

'Cariola,' said Hanno, sternly, 'he used to talk about worms. Worms are not wonderful.' It struck him that Aram ought to enjoy being dead. No one had taken his windy prophecies very seriously while he had been alive.

Cariola looked slyly at him. 'He said that the Shepherd would be a man who bleeds in the face.'

Hanno flushed, painfully. 'Only once – or twice.' *Would* bleed?

She gave him a fearsome dig in the ribs. 'Don't be silly. We all know how often it happens. There's no need to blush. You can't help it.'

Hanno's sudden tide of warmth ebbed as suddenly as it had come, and left him shuddering. Watched. Always.

He managed to say, 'Then it's not surprising that Aram knew too.' Then he thought, *Often?*

'But he said it before you came.'

'You're imagining that.'

'Oh no. Ask the others. They'll tell you.'

That's just what I'm afraid of. 'Cariola, he was mad. Not a prophet; never a prophet; he was mad.'

'Do you remember what Dow said, only a month or two back? That the greatest miracle worker of them all was thought to be a madman in his day.'

'When did Aram work his miracles?' Cariola fondled his hand, like a potter wedging clay, and then got up and waded to the doorway. 'He hasn't worked any miracles.'

'Not yet,' said Cariola, and wallowed out of his line of vision. Her voice drifted back across the sanctuary. 'Did you notice how many people came to the service, this morning? More than forty. I counted.'

At the noon service there were more than fifty, and after the evening service Cariola reported breathlessly that she had counted no less than seventy-two faithful worshippers assembled in the well of the temple. Hanno wondered if his father or Ivo had been among them, and for once hoped not.

'They only come because a man died here. It won't last,' he said, disgusted. He remembered a time, about three years ago, when a man had fallen from a barge near the Mill Bridge and never come up again. His friends had instantly dived after him, but they had brought him to the surface drowned. For hours afterwards, people had gathered on the bank, and the landing stage, lined the bridge and leaned out of windows, in order to see the place where a man had died.

'Is that where he went in?' Hanno had been asked, by a woman who brought along three small children to look.

'Yes. But he's been taken out already,' Hanno said. 'There's nothing to see. Unless you've never seen water before,' he added, spurred to insult by the woman's ugly curiosity. 'But it's not the same water. The water that drowned him is out to sea by now. This is just ordinary water, fresh out of the earth, that never drowned anyone. Not worth looking at at all.'

Was that same woman in the temple today? Was Ivo? Was Anise? He had forgotten Anise.

His disgust did not abate during the following days, when he saw that after the services a few people remained behind and, in the company of one of the Handmaidens, were shown the precise spot behind the altar where Aram's body had been discovered. The ambiguous basket was held up for inspection, and by the end of the week he noticed that he himself was being pointed out as the one who had found Aram dead, without a mark on him. After that, he took to loitering in the Robing Room until he could be fairly sure that the temple was empty and the gate locked. This last evasion made him smile, sadly. Not so long ago he had watched that gate, after services, in the hope that it might be left open.

One day Dow met him at the door of the Robing Room and told him that he was wanted by visitors. Could it be Father and Ivo at last? Following Dow, he went down to the well of the temple and there discovered three grave old men awaiting him with reverently bowed heads. Hanno felt a *frisson* of displeasure. When he wore the vestments of the Shepherd he was prepared to accept the reverence due to the Shepherd. Without the sheepskin and the head-dress he was only Hanno, worthy of nothing more than the commonplace courtesies that any man might expect.

'You are the Shepherd?' asked the one who seemed to be the eldest.

'Yes.' Hanno was disinclined to chop logic with men old enough to be his grandfathers. And if it pleased them it did him no harm.

'You are the man who found the prophet dead, with no mark on him?'

'Who?'

'We come from a village, many miles from here. Goat Lees, we call it.'

'I know Goat Lees.' That is; I know the girl at the tavern. That is, I knew. . .

'We heard that a prophet had died in the temple, and we have come to hear the truth.'

He looked with angry pity at the good old men, betrayed by rumour.

'I'll tell you the truth,' he began, vigorously. 'I found him and I knew him.' He got no further. Dow's right arm, disposed in amiable negligence about his neck, suddenly tightened, and equally suddenly, Hanno was smitten with an inexplicable pain along the length of his spine.

'Go on,' Dow said. 'They're waiting.'

'Are you unwell?' asked one of the old men, alarmed.

'He's all right,' said Dow. 'Sir. But remember, he has had a remarkable experience. He has not emerged unscathed.'

Bright dots, with tails, like little fish, swam briskly in at one eye and out of the other. Hanno breathed freely again and went on.

'His name was Aram and he said many – many – things – that we did not understand. He often spoke of his death. He said he would be found without a mark on him.'

'Tell them everything,' said Dow.

'He said, the sky would open like the mouth of the basilisk; the sand would run and run on that day. On the day of the worm. And he said his head would be c-c-c-cloven like a cheese, and his spirit would be taken up out of it, and there would be no mark on him. And, and. . .'

'The cleft,' said Dow.

'Yes. He said the cleft would close, and he would be found with no mark on him. And he was. Found. I found him.'

'And it was as he said?'

'Yes, but. . .'

'Just as he said,' Dow broke in. 'And that was not the only truth that he spoke, was it, Shepherd? He said, many months before the last Festival, that the Shepherd to come would be a man who bleeds in the face. And he does. He also said that he would be the most unwilling Shepherd the Temple had ever known.' Dow turned and smiled affectionately, full in Hanno's eyes. 'And he is.'

'I don't believe you,' Hanno bawled, in despair. 'I don't believe you. He never said a word about me before I came. I don't believe it.'

'How do you know what he said before you came?'

'He said you would bleed in the face,' said Nola. 'And we've all seen you.'

'Once or twice. Anyone's nose can bleed.'

'Anyone's nose can bleed,' Egil agreed. 'But yours never seems to stop. We've actually witnessed ten – oh yes, I know you've tried to hide them, I can't think why. Infirmity isn't a crime. I don't know how many others –'

'You count?'

'Yes, certainly.'

'You count my nose-bleeds?' His sense of the ridiculous almost got the better of him. 'How *repulsive*.'

'We wouldn't have done,' said Dow, 'only we knew what to expect – on account of what Aram said.'

'Ten? I don't believe ten.'

'At least ten, I said.'

'You're making it up. He never said anything about bleeding until he saw me.'

'Prove it, since you're so sure,' said Egil.

'I can't prove it – but I don't believe it.'

'You would say that,' said Egil. 'Just what do you believe; if anything?'

He found that he had been wrong about the interest excited by Aram's death. Cariola soon lost count of the numbers who attended the services, and the first few visitors to the back of the altar, bareheaded and piously carrying their shoes, soon swelled to the proportions of a mass pilgrimage, in spite of the fact that the Book forbade the unsanctified to enter the sanctuary. Cariola and Nola acquired new, austere dresses, and went very solemnly about their job of guiding the pilgrims. Discreet attempts were made to tidy the temple. These came to nothing since the official cleaners, Hanno's old harridan among them, had defected months ago and the job could not properly be given to anyone else since all duties were firmly designated by the Book. However, the uneven stones in the courtyard were taken up and reset, and the gutter that crossed it was cleaned out. A potter was sent for to replace the broken tiles in the well. Hanno was returning from the bath house when he was told that the potter wanted to see him.

'To see me?' Another innocent seeking confirmation of the prophet's death. 'Well, I don't want to see him.'

'It's your brother,' said Frey, who had brought the message.

'Ivo?'

'He didn't give a name,' said Frey. 'He told me he wanted to see his brother the Shepherd, so I suppose he is the Shepherd's brother.'

Hanno looked down into the well and saw Ivo in close conversation with Dow and Egil.

'Go on down,' said Frey.

'Couldn't I see him in the garden?' said Hanno. 'Alone?'

'See him where you like, so long as you don't take him into the Hut,' said Frey.

Hanno was fully prepared to find himself entertaining Dow and Egil as well, but they moved away as he approached. He came up behind Ivo and touched him on the shoulder, almost timidly. Once he would have run at him, Guardians or no Guardians, seized him, swung him round and hugged him. After his trip home he was too inhibited to do any of these things, in case Ivo tore himself away and started bowing.

'Ivo?'

His brother turned and stared at him, a stare full of discomfort and uncertainty. Hanno looked down, shyly.

'I wish you had come before.'

'I am so happy to see you,' said Ivo, formally.

'I should hope so. Let's go into the garden. It's quiet there.'

'If you wish.' Ivo joined his fingers and lowered his head over the linked hands.

'Oh, don't do that, don't *do* that,' Hanno pleaded. He almost dragged Ivo out of the temple, down the steps and into the garden. He closed the iron gate behind them and they sat down on a bench by the brick path. Hanno settled astride it, facing his brother. Ivo looked straight ahead.

'By now you should have become accustomed to obeisance,' he said. 'You should learn to receive it gracefully.'

'I don't like to see my big brother bowing and scraping over me.'

'It's your due, as the Shepherd.'

'I'm not the Shepherd. Inside that temple is a place they call the Robing Room. The Shepherd lives in there. He is a belt, a jerkin and a head-dress. He only comes to life when I put him on, and I am nothing without him.'

'Then why do you suppose,' said Ivo, still not looking at him, 'that they go to so much trouble to Choose the Shepherd?'

'Because the Book tells them to,' said Hanno. 'If they really cared who wore the vestments they certainly wouldn't choose like that. They wouldn't have chosen me for a start.'

'The god Chooses,' said Ivo.

'All right, we won't argue, but if that's so, the god doesn't care either.'

'But it was foretold that you would become Shepherd,' said Ivo. 'Everyone knows.'

'Stop that!' Hanno said, sharply. 'That's Guardians' talk. I won't hear it from you. Oh Ivo, why didn't you come sooner? I wanted so much. . .' He stopped and hung his head. 'You said you'd pray that I wasn't chosen. You didn't, did you?'

'How could I? It was prophesied –'

'No.'

'All over the city they are saying it. Everyone knows.'

'But you surely don't believe it,' said Hanno. 'Come on, tell me, when did you first hear about this prophecy? Five minutes ago, wasn't it? From my two dear Friends back there?'

'I told you, it's all over the city.'

'I heard you. But when did *you* first know?'

'Soon after you came here,' said Ivo. Hanno rocked back and only just saved himself from falling off the bench.

'No you didn't.'

'Or it may have been before.'

'It was not.'

'No, you're right. It was just after.'

'Ivo, you sweet fool, I only heard it myself a few weeks ago.'

'It was a great comfort to Father, after you'd been Chosen.'

'He didn't need comforting. I saw him in the winter. He couldn't get me out of the house fast enough, and he definitely didn't mention any prophecy. Anyway, I never had a nose-bleed in my life, before I came here.'

'Who's talking about nose-bleeds?' said Ivo, genuinely perplexed. 'The prophet said that the next Shepherd would live in fear of death by water.'

Hanno laughed; just. 'But Ivo, remember – god, it's not yet nine months ago – how can you have forgotten? I wasn't afraid of water. I used to work on a boat.'

'They say you're afraid of it now,' said Ivo.

'Who says I'm afraid of water?' he shouted. He forgot the secret knowledge and grabbed Dow by the front of his tunic. 'What have you been saying to my brother? What nonsense have you been telling him? He even believes it.'

'Let go of me or I'll make you,' said Dow, his self-control growing in proportion to Hanno's helpless rage. 'You know I can make you, and there are three others here who can do it just as well. Why pretend that you aren't afraid of water? It's so obvious. Even people who hardly know you have mentioned it.'

'But he never mentioned it. Aram never said so.'

'You won't go to the bath house if anyone else is there. You go out fast, if anyone comes in. You sit on the edge of the fountain and shake.'

'I lived on the river. I had a boat – I worked on that boat, it was my living. I dived, I swam –'

'If we took you to the river now, would you dive? Would you swim?'

'When did Aram ever come into the bath house? He never saw me by the fountain.'

'Of course he didn't. He didn't need to. He knew.'

'He did not.'

'Shall we take you to the river?'

'He never said it. *He never said it!*'

The priest floated among them, very much perturbed.

'My children: brawling in the Temple: is this pleasing to the god?'

Dow and the Guardians knelt. Hanno was shocked by his outburst, but he could see that they were shocked by the sacrilege.

He thought, They really believe that the god is offended. Where is this offended spirit, and what is he doing about it?

'You must atone. Beg forgiveness. Subdue the Spirit.'

'Oh, no, not another onion,' Hanno snarled, without thinking. The priest turned on him.

'Speak not so of it. It is the Bread of Mortification.'

'*It's a sodding onion!*'

The priest slapped his face. It was not a hard blow, and the priest had to stand on tiptoe to deliver it, but Hanno gathered that he had overstepped the mark, this time. Dow and the Guardians looked up from their grovelling with expressions of utter amazement.

'Your tongue should wither at the root,' said the priest, in a little, exhausted voice. 'Very well, if you object to eating the Bread of Mortification, you shall eat nothing at all. For two days.'

He shuffled down the steps and across the well. Hanno watched him go with profound relief, but had the wit not to show it. At that moment, even starving to death seemed preferable to eating an onion, and there was no Aram now to help him.

'For that you would have been flayed, once,' said Dow.

'Once,' said Hanno.

'The priest should have beaten you.'

'He couldn't,' said Hanno.

The Guardians stood up. 'We could,' they said.

PART THREE

Summer

11

THIS time he *had* overstepped the mark. All his efforts to curb his tongue counted for nothing beside his impious insult to the onion. He was given to understand that since he could not be trusted to speak nicely, he need not speak at all, and nobody spoke to him. For three weeks he was left to keep his own company and discovered that it was less congenial than it used to be. No one addressed him, no one came near him.

All the same, when he sat in the Hut, he sometimes noticed a slight tumescence in the tent-cloth, as though someone were leaning lightly on the other side. Every time he came out of a doorway he thought he saw the dusty whisk of a skirt or a caftan in the corner of his eye. When he went to the bath house he was conscious that he was never alone in the slype. A door would open or close. When he reached the cistern the water was disturbed. More than once he collided with a figure in the dark.

The figure should have cried out, or cursed his clumsiness, but it never spoke until one day an almost recognized voice murmured in the soft blackness, close to his ear:

'The prophet said that the Shepherd would be afraid of the dark.'

Hanno had his hand safely on the door knob, so he was able to pause long enough to reply, 'Then he was wrong. I'm not afraid of the dark.'

'Not yet,' said the voice.

He went out into the temple, lily, rose, mallow, hemlock, spurge, seeing nothing but taking a path that his feet knew.

He was almost halfway round behind the altar before he realized which way he was going, rose, hemlock, sorrel, and by then he was nearing Aram's untenanted den. A movement made him look up and he saw people kneeling behind the altar. For a moment he thought he had lost his wits. Nowadays there were always people behind the altar, after a service. But there had been no service.

Or had there been a service and he had missed it?

Or had he attended the service and not noticed it? He couldn't remember what time of day it was, morning, noon, or evening. He leaned against a column and looked at the clerestories, searching for the sun. It was behind him: after noon. He looked for shadows: long: long after noon. He thought of the sand clock in the priest's room, turning, turning, playing the same hour over and over again.

There had been no service. Yes.

No.

There had been a service, hours ago. Where had he been since then? In the bath house? Five minutes at most. Before that? In the Hut, where else? Perhaps sleeping. Sleeping was the only thing he could look forward to, now, so long as he didn't dream. Maybe he was dreaming; walking in his sleep.

One of the figures leaned over and nudged another. He heard a whispered warning.

'It's the Shepherd.' They all stood up, bowed, and stood up again.

Women.

They came towards him, moving noiselessly over the tiles. He put out his arms behind him and clasped the column.

'Who are you?'

'The Crier came out and called to us, and we came here,' said one.

The Crier? Then he remembered Dow, complaining.

'They send out the Crier, and no one comes. I remember my mother, my aunts, used to put on their best clothes to clean the Temple. They would leave the house singing and work all day.'

He looked again and began to smile, ashamed of himself. He saw seven nice ladies who had come to clean the temple; and one old harridan who had defected and returned, she who had woken him with a mop on cloudy mornings. The seven ladies and the harridan smiled back.

'We were looking at the place where the prophet died,' said one. Hanno's smile broke. Two months ago, the Crier could have walked the city streets all day, and shouted himself hoarse, and no one would have come.

By the end of the week there were thirty-three ladies and seventeen old harridans at work on the temple.

'There'll be one of you for each tile soon,' said Hanno, and was informed that the prophet had foretold exactly the number of women who would honour the god by labouring in his temple.

'Tell me another,' said Hanno. He counted again, three days later, and found that there were still fifty. One way or another, Aram's estimate was being proved accurate. Hanno could not recall that Aram had ever given much thought to the state of the floor. After all, he had been perfectly satisfied with his squalid sett behind the altar.

The tiles shone like ice and felt like glass. One day, coming in from the courtyard and wearing sandals, Hanno went into a long, uncontrolled skid and slid for several yards before he shunted into Dow. They were both so surprised that they laughed, and the fractured friendship went some way towards being repaired.

'You were better off barefoot,' said Dow. 'I wish I could leave off my boots.'

It was a cack-handed remark, and obviously untrue.

Hanno supposed that he was making an effort at reconciliation, told himself that he had behaved abominably and, for a few minutes, thought that it was very kind of Dow to make any effort at all.

As he climbed the steps he paused to let a woman walk across his path with a garland of spring flowers. She pattered round the colonnade and went behind the altar. Hanno hesitated to follow her. Instead he slipped off his sandals and went round the other way, across the sanctuary and past the Hut. He moved stealthily, and by the time he arrived the woman had gone, leaving the wreath behind her. He waited until she was out of sight and went forwards, kneeling to look into the gloomy cavern where Aram had made his home.

Something quite different had been made of it since he last looked. The rubbish heap where Aram had burrowed like a maggot in an apple had been pushed to one side, where it had collapsed upon its hollow self. In its place stood a new structure, on tiles that had been swept and scoured and burnished with beeswax. The derelict hurdles were displaced by a trellis of fresh white wood, overlaid by a felt cloth instead of the threadbare tapestry. An iron bracket had been hung to one side and in it a little lamp of scented oil burned without flickering. By its light Hanno saw a low ascetic couch, covered by a spotless quilt, where Aram had spread his ragged palliasse. A new earthenware ewer replaced the chipped flagon, an orderly thatcher's sheaf of reeds was propped against the wall. Hanno looked round for the broken basket, over which he was said to have fallen, and found it lying at the foot of the couch, transformed into a wicker trug; and lying in it, the remnant of the god's garment, a snowy linen napkin hemmed with intricate gold stitches. In the middle of the floor lay the wreath, a pristine apology for the garland that Aram had woven from dead flowers, and thrust through the wreath like an arrow through a heart, was an oak staff, tipped with a ram's horn, such as the Shepherd himself carried; no besoms here.

It was the cell of an anchorite; a clean respectable place that any clean respectable prophet would be happy to own. What pure thoughts might not a pure man think in a place like this?

Hanno backed out and knew at once that he was being watched. He looked round and saw no one, but from the darkness behind the prophet's cell, a single eye watched him without intelligence. It was the tapestry, tossed aside to return to the decay from which Aram had briefly resurrected it: the dying ram, forever transfixed by the knife at its throat.

He stood up and ran roselilywoodbinesorrelroseroserose over the railing and into the Hut.

He was forgiven. The priest laid a forgetful hand on his head; Cariola smiled at him; Dow, smelling strongly of onions, offered him a choice bone to gnaw at supper. Hanno bowed to the priest, smiled at Cariola, accepted the bone and wondered what they were after.

Later they sat companionably on the turf in the windless garden, to enjoy the last of the evening sun. Nola and Cariola made a chain of daisies, a dozen to each link. Dow and Egil and Frey brought out a smooth tile and a bag of copper coins. One coin lay in the centre of the tile and they took turns to tip it into a cup, using a second coin as a lever.

Hanno declined their offer to let him play and lay back on the turf, listening to the small sounds that passed for silence. He rested one arm across his eyes, seeing daisies like white stars drift through the darkness. The pinking coins reminded him of finches. From time to time an insect alighted on his arm or face and he let it rest, feeling too reposeful to disrupt anything, even the vagaries of an insect.

Lying there, flat, quite still, he thought he felt the earth move under him. Perhaps Aram had been right and it was the world that turned while the sky stood still. When he lay on his couch at night and watched the sliding stars cross the clerestories, he wondered, Who moves? As he lay here, feeling the sun slip away from his face, he could have sworn that it was the earth that tilted and he felt himself swung vertiginously up and over, until he fell away from the sun, into a black abyss where there was neither up nor down. He clutched at the grass with his other hand, to keep himself from rolling.

'Do you remember how the Prophet used to come here?' said Nola. Hanno began to turn his head, almost opened his eyes, but checked himself. I didn't hear that.

'He loved this garden,' said Cariola. He thought, How pink her voice is: the most foolish colour.

'It was evenings like this that he loved most. I often saw him sitting here when the light was fading.'

'He felt at one with the god,' said Frey. Now Frey rarely said anything. He sounded as though he were reciting a verse of the Book, painfully memorized.

Aram's visits to the garden had been restricted to furtive raids on the rubbish heap, to gather wilted blossoms for his garlands. Hanno, once pitying what he took to be Aram's hopeless striving after beauty, had removed a particularly fine white lily from one of Cariola's garlands and presented it to him to put in his own. Aram had inspected it in total bewilderment, failed to identify it as anything within his canon, and dropped it in the dust. Hanno, disheartened, had let it lie, but three days later, when the lily had become a limp rag, decaying silkily, Aram had retrieved it and worn it behind his ear.

'It was here that he first spoke about the Worm,' said Egil.

'The Day of the Worm,' said Nola.

'On that Day the Shepherd shall find me dead with no mark on me,' said Frey. Without doubt, he was reciting.

Hanno refused to move, to react. He lay quite motionless, his arm pressed over his eyes, and knew that they were all watching him.

'The most unwilling Shepherd the Temple has ever known.'

'Who fears death by water.'

'Who fears the dark.'

'Who bleeds in the face.'

Just like lines of the Book, painfully memorized. Was this how the rituals had grown, year after year, time out of mind, a patent falsifying of accounts, the erasure of truth from the records? Instead of being a mere passing Shepherd, one among hundreds, he was being written in, absorbed. He was no longer the faceless figure who wore the head-dress and the sheepskin and the belt. He was acquiring attributes. He would be remembered.

I don't want to be remembered. When my time is up I want to leave. I don't want to leave anything behind, not even a memory. I should have passed through here like water.

Another insect settled on his hand, traversed the ruts of his knuckles and began to wander on the causeway of his wrist. Round it went, on feathery feet. It would not go away. Annoyed by the tickling he opened his eyes and looked sideways down the vista of his arm. A bracelet of daisies encircled his wrist. Cariola had taken one end of the chain and slipped it over his hand.

'I thought you were asleep,' she said, fondly. 'You were lying so still.'

'No.' No, you didn't think I was asleep.

'Where shall I put the other end?' said Nola. She paced the narrow turf, casting about for somewhere to hang the daisy chain that trailed behind her, looping and twitching on the blades of grass, tugging feebly but firmly against his skin. An old iron ring hung from the wall where perhaps a dog had once been tethered. 'Here we are.' Nola opened the last link of the chain, threaded it through the ring and closed it again. She turned to smile at Hanno. 'Now you can't get away.'

He looked at his hand and saw another chain, as insubstantial as daisies: unbreakable. Words.

'You think not?' He scrambled up and jerked contemptuously at the daisy chain. By some natural perversity it did not break. He stood looking at it stupidly, and they all smiled.

'The Shepherd shall be afraid of flowers.'

Frey turned to Egil. 'Did the Prophet say that?'

'No,' said Egil. 'I said that.'

'Shepherd!' Egil was calling across the well. 'Shepherd!'

He was resigned now, to the loss of his name. Not even Dow used it any more and after all, why should he? The Shepherd was the Shepherd. He still muttered to himself, My name is Hanno, but the very sound of the name rang false, as if it had ceased to have any value of its own. The ritual had taken everything of him that was needed, and discarded his name, which was not. He crossed the well to where Egil was standing.

'The Priest has sent for you.'

'What have I done?'

'Nothing, so far as I know,' said Egil. 'Why assume that you've done anything – unless you have. I shouldn't care to have your conscience,' he said.

'Then why does he want me?'

Egil shrugged, as though this were a whim beyond his comprehension. 'He'll see you now,' he said. Hanno went down the passage to the priest's door, knocked and went in. He entered on the hour. The sand clock turned. Another hour began to slide away. The priest stood up to greet him.

'My son.'

'Sir?'

'It lacks only five weeks to the Festival. What shall be done then, my son?'

'You let me go,' said Hanno.

'It will seem very strange without you,' said the priest.

'You will have another Shepherd,' said Hanno. 'A better one, I hope.'

'Of course. There is always another Shepherd, and another, and another. But for many of us you have become *the* Shepherd. You were Chosen.'

'I thought all Shepherds were chosen.'

'Sit down,' said the priest. He did not offer a chair so Hanno sat on the floor, instantly at a disadvantage. 'My son, we knew of your Coming before you Came. The Prophet told us.'

'Aram.'

'That was his name, while he was among us, but he has been Taken Up, as he foretold, without a mark on him. You found him without a mark on him.'

'Yes.' Yes yes yes.

'But we were deaf; we were blind. We did not know that we looked upon a Prophet. We did not know that we heard the Words of the god. But you opened our eyes; you opened our ears. You were sent to show us the Truth.'

Hanno found that his mouth had fallen open, and chucked it shut with the heel of his hand. He wanted to say, *You* don't believe this crap, do you? but he desisted. Belief was something he knew very little about. If an educated old man could believe in an unseen god that did nothing to manifest itself, why should he not believe that a lunatic spoke truly of the future, and that a young man who suffered from heavy nose-bleeds should be the object of divine appointment. He had been told what he wanted to hear and he wanted to believe it. Hanno could guess who had told him. Well, if they were so desperate for a miracle that they would accept Aram as a prophet, it was not his concern. In five weeks he would be out of it. Let them harass and haunt him. In five weeks he would be gone, and they could start all over again with someone else.

'I'm glad I was instrumental in showing you the truth,' he said.

'It was Inevitable,' said the priest. 'You were the One for whom we were Waiting.'

Hanno did not care for the sound of this. 'But you will let me go?' he said, unable to withold that plea. He had nothing to lose now, by appearing unwilling. Never mind what the Book said about the Shepherd becoming willing, to fulfil their prophecy he must remain unwilling. They wanted most piously that he should be unwilling. When did they first realize just how unwilling he was? The day he ran away from Dow, presumably. Or had it been sooner? Had they all shared his secret, all along?

Not possible.

'Of course we shall let you go,' said the priest, benevolently. 'But you have a duty to perform first.'

'A duty to whom?' he asked, suspiciously.

'First of all, to the god in his Temple, of course; but also to the people. Since the Prophet was Taken Up, the people have remembered the god, and turned aside from their backsliding. Do you not owe it to them to hold up a lamp that shall show them the way?'

'I'll hold up a lamp,' said Hanno, relaxing again.

'Good. Then listen to me, and I shall tell you exactly what you must do.' He leaned forward and revealed to his horrified Shepherd the exact nature of the lamp he was to hold up.

Then he sent him away.

*

Dow and Frey were on duty, playing at statues in the colonnade, but Egil was somewhere about. Cariola and Nola were somewhere about. Hanno dodged from column to column, seeking a hiding-place, but the temple was alive with cleaners plying across the tiles with mops, like bumboats in a harbour. One of them was even beating the dust out of his own tent-cloth with a wooden paddle. He looked across the courtyard towards the gate; it was closed and locked. No visitors. One place at least would be private. He went to the altar, as reluctant to enter the Prophet's Cell in its embalmed cleanliness as he had once been for quite a different reason; but there was nowhere else.

As he went by the altar something caught his eye, and he went back for a second look. At the foot of Aram's favourite vase there lay something that he took, at first, to be a live creature, about three inches long, narrow, grey, curled back on itself in the serpentine curve of a pot hook. It was lying quite still. He touched it with a fingernail and it moved, all of a piece, beneath the pressure. It was made of clay. It was a worm.

He picked it up, more repelled than he would have been were it alive, and inspected it. It was roughly fashioned, tapered at one end to indicate a tail, and with two small depressions at the other, like rudimentary eyes. He had seen little clay tablets appear before on the altar. Inscribed with the earnest wishes of the donor, they were put there to attract the attention of the god; votive offerings. This was a votive worm.

The damage was done. The poison had reached the people. He replaced the worm, circled the altar and ducked in at the entrance to the Prophet's Cell. A curtain hung discreetly over the doorway; To keep out the dust, he sneered to himself; however, it afforded him the privacy that he could find nowhere else. He hardly liked to lie on the bed, so he sat once more on the floor and unrolled the sheet of parchment that the priest had given him. On it, in the priest's own exquisite cursive, was the priest's own contribution to the Festival, that Hanno must utter in the name of the Shepherd. He broke out in a sweat at the thought of it, at the vision of himself clad in his belt and sheepskin, and his bestial head-dress, mouthing this apocalyptic drivel. And he had to learn it by heart.

He held the parchment flat on the tiles and lowered his head over it. Even allowing for the dim light he found the writing terribly difficult to read. He was out of practice and his eyes were out of alignment. The characters straggled across the page like ravelled threads, and it was not until his nose was almost touching them that he could knit them into words. He knew that this should worry him, but there were more urgent matters to engage him.

I am the Shepherd, Chosen by the god, who Stands before the god and Calls upon him in the name of the people.

*I am the Shepherd of whom it was said. . .*I can't say this; it's bad enough reading it; I can't say it. . .*He shall bleed in the face. He shall fear death by water. He shall fear the dark* – which I don't – *He shall be the most unwilling Shepherd that the Temple has ever known.*

These are the Words of the Prophet who knew me before I came.

*And the Prophet said to the Shepherd. . .*It's inhuman. No one should have to do this. . .*said to the Shepherd, When the Day of the Worm Cometh, the sky shall open like the mouth of the Basilisk, and my Head shall be cloven like a cheese, and my Spirit shall be Taken Up and the cleft shall close and there shall be No Mark on me.*

The Day of the Worm has Come, and the Prophet has been Taken Up, and there was No Mark on him. The Shepherd has seen this thing and knows that it is true. Do they really think it's true? Do they, come to that, think that

I think it's true, or do they just want me to do their lying for them? The Shepherd speaks to the god in the name of the people – and to the people in the name of the god. They know I shall be believed. Yes, they want me to do their lying for them.

He saw at last where his dissembling had brought him. They thought he would do anything they wanted, and they were very nearly right. He had been doing what they wanted for almost eleven months, all those times he had almost told the truth and then withheld it, for the sake of peace. This was his reward; not peace.

Then the Priest shall say: All who have gathered here, listen to the Shepherd tell of the Miracle.

And the Shepherd shall say: It was told me by the Prophet that I should find him Dead with No Mark on him. And so did I find him.

Priest: And where did you find him?

Shepherd: I found him by the Altar where he Dwelt, serving the god, living in the Most Holy Place.

Priest: And what did he hold in his Hand?

Shepherd: In one Hand he did hold the Vessel of Sacrifice and in the other he did hold the Remnant of the god's Garment. . .No, that's too much. It was a floor-cloth. Everyone knew that.

They think they can beat me into submission. They needn't. Five weeks and I'll be gone. I don't care any more. That first day, when the priest took hold of me and shook me. . .I should have struck him down on the spot. Then there would have been no Shepherd. Only me. . .

Priest: And you looked upon him?

Shepherd: And I looked upon him.

Priest: And he Fell in your sight?

Shepherd: And he Fell in my sight.

Priest: He was then Dead?

Shepherd: He was then Dead.

Priest: With No Mark on him?

Shepherd: With No Mark on him.

Then the Priest shall say: His Head was Cloven open and he was Taken Up by the hand of the god, and there was No Mark on him.

Hanno closed his eyes and banged his head on the floor. I can't do this. Too late he heard the approaching voices. The curtain was jerked aside and there stood Nola, with a stout lady visitor. If anything, she was more surprised than he was. The curtain was dropped again and he heard her explaining, 'That was the Shepherd, praying at the Shrine of the Prophet.'

Oh; it's a shrine now, is it?

The stout lady's sigh fluttered the curtain. 'What a charming young man; but so pale! Does the ritual insist that he bang his head on the floor? It seems very hard, and it can't do him any good...' The voice sighed into silence.

'Oh no,' said Nola, moving away. 'He doesn't have to do it. But he is so very devout...'

12

HE absented himself from the midday meal and walked in the garden, learning his lines and swearing that he would never say them.

*And the Prophet said to the Shepherd, When the Day of the Worm Cometh, the sky shall open. . .*I could refuse.

I could tell them, If you want a miracle, make your own.

They have made their miracle. Aram the fool has become Aram the Holy Fool. Now I have to endorse it. I am the witness; why does it have to be me?

Because I found him. And because I will be believed.

If I hadn't run from them that day, someone else would have found him. Dow or Cariola would be the witness. Cariola was the closest, she saw me fall over his foot – no. She saw me fall over the basket. I'm sure it was his foot. I'm sure she thought it was his foot at first. If she saw so much, let her be witness.

But Aram never spoke to her; he only spoke to me. And they heard.

I saw nothing. If only they knew how little I can see. It's too late to tell them now.

I won't do it.

From the roof of the temple a foreshortened figure looked down at him. He saw it as an ethereal smear against the sky.

Who's that? Aram on his way down again, to see how we're getting on without him?

The figure busied itself with clanging and ringing. Hanno gathered that it was a workman of some kind, repairing the slates. Since attendance at the services had revived, there was suddenly more maintenance carried out, more money to pay for the maintenance. Two other workers joined the first, and Hanno heard the gnats' hum of their conversation.

How did they get up there?

There were no stairs. He walked to the middle of the garden and looked up, over the bean rows and vines, to the back of the temple. A gigantic ladder of scaffolding spanned the fifty feet between the ground and the roof; a hundred beams and spars that stood between the temple and the wall. On the way up the scaffolding passed the top of the wall. On the other side of the wall was the river. Anyone who climbed the scaffolding could step off, just there, poise himself on the wall's top and dive, and the river would take him safely.

Hanno smiled a little bitterly. After all this time, an escape route, and he no longer needed it. Once he would have searched and probed until he found his way to the foot of that great ladder and climbed and dived.

And they would have followed him, and fetched him and brought him back. Or the city would have sent him back – for good luck. Now he had only a few weeks to endure and he could walk out of the gate, and no one would bring him back. After he had testified to the miraculous death of the Prophet.

In one Hand he did hold the Vessel of Sacrifice and in the other he did hold the Remnant...

His eye wandered towards the scaffolding.

I won't do it.

What do you suppose they will do if you refuse; smile and say all right, and forget about it? Suppose they don't let me go – they couldn't do that. Everyone expects a new Shepherd after the Festival. The Book demands it. Father and Ivo would...

Oh yes? What would Father and Ivo do? Even they

believe the prophecy now. Can I be the only one who doesn't believe it? Egil said, Just what do you believe? Does he know what he meant? Do I? Does Nola really imagine that I knock my head on the floor in ecstacy? I should never have pretended to believe in the first place. I should have said, Look, all this is nothing to me, but I don't want to spoil it for anyone else. I'll do what's needed.

Dow says Aram said I was unwilling. Aram never said that to me. Or did he? Dow must know. They all know. What will they do to me?

My head aches.

I won't do it.

'Dow?'

'Shepherd?'

'Wouldn't it be more impressive if one of you bore witness to the miracle; at the Festival?'

'But you found him.'

'We all found him.'

'You were the first. Remember, you said, He's dead. Then you said, Did I do it?'

'Yes, I remember. But I don't think I can say truly what happened. I don't remember very much, and I didn't see –'

'You were upset.'

'Everyone remembers that.'

'Anyway, you have only to say what the Priest has written. It's written down exactly as it happened.'

'Is it?'

'Oh, yes. Every word of it is true.'

They were standing at the end of the cookhouse next to the little window, with its tiny warped panes. Outside, as seen through water, one massive leg of the scaffolding rose into the dusk.

Dow followed Hanno's eyes, up, up.

'You can't get at it,' he said. 'There's no way out there that you know of. Go back to your Hut, Shepherd, and learn your testimony.'

The worms proliferated.

'They're breeding,' said Hanno, counting more than a dozen on the altar. Cariola, who stood nearby, flushed a deeper pink than usual and murmured of sacrilege. The first worms, being made of rude, unfired clay, soon crumbled and had to be removed by one of the equally numerous ladies, using a little silver-backed brush and salver, specially provided for that purpose, but within a few days a more highly evolved species appeared among the fleeces. These were a sophisticated race, glazed, with a potter's mark underneath. The first were self-coloured and smooth; featureless. Their descendants were marvellously wrought, segmented, textured, ornamented in glowing colours no annelid ever owned.

How did they get there? Hanno imagined them gliding ventrally across the tiles in the damp dusk, and slithering up the front of the altar at midnight. Apart from those who came to clean, no layman was allowed beyond the sanctuary railing unaccompanied, and he was assailed by another vision of the importunate worshippers leaning over the rail and shying their worms at the altar like hoop-la players at a fair.

Then he noticed that before each service taut ropes, like washing-lines across an alley, were strung between columns facing the courtyard. As the worshippers entered the temple, those who had a worm with them hung it by the tail from one of the ropes. At every service there were more worshippers, and one evening he reckoned that there must be upwards of a hundred worms swaying in the breeze and jingling faintly, making sweet worm music that chimed above the coarser cadences of the temple band.

Cariola and Nola gathered them up, and distributed them on the altar. Each worm was allowed to try its luck for a week before being moved on to an unknown destination. The girls were punctilious about arranging them in strict order of precedence, so that no worm might get more or less time under the god's eye than another.

From wondering how they arrived, he started to wonder where they came from. The potters' marks were legion. Clearly there was a worm boom in the city. Did the potters send out peddlars, crying their wares about the streets? 'Worms! Worms! Fine worms! Get your worms here!' Would any potter do such a thing? Would Ivo? He began to search for Ivo's mark among the worms, and when he found it he sat for a whole afternoon in the Hut, and would not speak, staring like an idiot at anyone who addressed him. He was thought to be meditating.

One day he observed that instead of pouring through the gate and across the courtyard, many worshippers were silting up in a corner by the gateway. As always, he was unable to go and look, since he was supposed to be on show in the sanctuary as soon as the gate opened, but after the rite had begun he found time to look out, beyond the colonnade, to the gate. A trestle table had been set up there, and a man was sitting at it with what appeared to be an abacus. An associate was packing something away in straw and trampling a number of empty boxes under foot. On the table a few highly coloured objects lay scattered. Hanno's eyesight was not equal to the distance, but it needed no stretch of the imagination to work out what was on sale.

Several of the common stock cleaners wore amulets about their necks, on cords: the worm again, writhen into a double ring to denote ecstasy, or to prevent it from slipping off the cord. The lady who dusted the altar of worm casts had a silver one on a silver chain. Gold worms with garnet eyes rose and fell on fervently heaving bosoms during the services, and vermiform barrettes with jewelled pins stuck through them peeped surprisingly from curls and chignons, like evidence of a nasty infestation.

The next time he went before the priest he had a proposition.

'Have you yet learned the Rite of the Death of the Prophet, my son?'

Have I not? 'Yes, I've learned it. But surely, there is no need for it at the Festival. Nothing will keep people away now. The place is craw – full of them. Everyone is wearing worms.'

'Serpents, my son.'

'I thought worms.'

'You are in error, my son. The Prophet foretold the Day of the Serpent, and the people wear the sign of the Serpent in honour of that Day.'

Hanno thought he had the advantage, for once.

'Aram told me he would die on the day of the worm. He never said anything about serpents.'

'Your memory is sadly at fault,' said the priest. 'We all know that the worm is the symbol of death and decay. Would the Prophet have spoken of worms?'

'Why not? He was foretelling his death.'

'The Serpent is the symbol of Mystery, of strength without stature –'

Yes, and now I know where you got your serpent from.

'– he walks upon his belly, without feet.'

'Like a worm.'

'You are the Shepherd. You should know, better than anyone, that the people are as sheep. They must be led. Within even your lifetime we have seen strange cults grow up. Has no one ever told you of the River Worship, and the false teacher from the north, who led the people astray? Men were instructed to throw their most cherished possessions into the river, to be taken to the god. The things that floated by...' He lost the thread of his discourse and meandered away on a current of reminiscence.

Hanno prompted him. 'And?'

'And the friends of the false teacher stood downstream with nets. The people must be shown that this Prophet is the true Prophet, and you must show them.'

He went back to his Hut and consulted the priest's manuscript, which he kept on the shelf under his table beside the letters and the leaf.

It says *worms. When the Day of the Worm Cometh... The Day of the Worm has Come.* I know it says worms.

It did not.

The ink that the priest used was thick and slab. When it dried it flaked. By inserting a fingernail under a letter, the letter could be prised away from the parchment, and someone had removed the word *worm* by doing just this. Faint traces of it were still discernable, even to Hanno, under the word that had replaced it, whose letters were cramped together so that it would fit into the space available.

When the Day of the Serpent Cometh...The Day of the Serpent has Come.

They think I won't notice. Then they do know how little I can see.

Why pretend?

Why did the Prophet never say that the Shepherd would be sand-blind?

Because the Shepherd had to see the Prophet dead, without a mark on him.

And the Shepherd saw nothing of the sort.

The Shepherd saw nothing at all.

And they know it.

Only, no one else must know it. *Bastards.*

Hanno raked the parchment with all five nails outspread until his lap was stippled with black flakes like soot, and the manuscript said nothing of worms or serpents; and what was true, and what was not, had gone without trace.

As he sat on the couch, tearing the parchment into tiny wafers, Egil and Dow came in and sat one on each side of him. They were very subservient. It seemed that they were there to apologize for something. He tried to pay attention to them, turning his eyes right and left, without moving his head, so as not to arouse the lurking pain inside. A fiddle-string twanged between one eye and the other. He knew what was going to happen and prayed that Egil and Dow would go away before it did, but they sat there, like ornamental urns on a wall, full of rubbish instead of flowers rose lily sorrel clover rose. . .

For the third time they broke it to him gently that the priest had received a deputation from the chief burgesses; headed by his father, as it happened. It was wonderful, really, when you came to think about it. People no longer felt that three services a day were enough – they felt the need to come before the god more often.

Yes, he said. Wonderful.

Which will mean leaving the gate open more often.

Yes.

You do understand, don't you, Shepherd?

Yes.

We know you wouldn't, of course, but

You do understand?

Yes. Yes. Perfectly.

The gate will be open for an hour every day
(Can't be watching you *all* the time)
starting now
it's not that
we don't
don't you
do you
see, don't you?

He scraped the words away and they fell like soot in his lap.

'It's only for an hour,' said Egil. 'Come on.'

'I don't think he heard you,' said Dow, in a tiny distant voice, like a bat in the roof. They led him to a small room in the priest's quarters with a small stool and a small sand clock for company, or comfort, or something less kindly intended.

'Get him a towel,' said the bat, faintly. 'He's going to need it.'

He held the towel against his face and watched the fiddle-string drawn finer than a hair until it broke. It was some time before he realized that they had locked him in.

'I suppose it would be foolish to suggest a walk?'

'Why? I'd be pleased to walk with you,' said Dow. 'In the garden?'

'In the city?'

Dow looked honestly hurt. 'Why do you make things so hard for yourself? You know the Priest won't allow it.'

'Why should I know that? The Book says that the Shepherd may go out if accompanied.'

'It's a pity you never read the Book. You'd save yourself a lot of trouble,' said Dow. 'The Book says that the Shepherd may not go out unaccompanied.'

'I dare say there's a difference, though I don't see it. Why won't the priest allow it?'

Dow shuffled his feet. 'Because of last time.'

'That was months ago,' said Hanno. 'Do you think I would do it again, after what you did to me? Does no one get a second chance?' Dow said nothing. Hanno answered for him. 'Yes, most people get a second chance, but I'm not one of them. I told you, I wasn't trying to escape from the temple. I wanted to come home alone. Why don't you believe me?'

Dow glowed with discomfort. 'It seems that you aren't always certain...You don't always know what you're saying.'

'Oh, I do.'

'It seems not, sometimes. You don't remember things that have happened. You don't even know they're happening, part of the time.'

'Is that how it seems?'

'Yes. I wish you wouldn't make me say these things. Sometimes you sound like an unbeliever – I don't mean that you are. We all know that.'

'Do you?'

'But you argue about the Prophecies. Why should you be right and the rest of us wrong? There are more than a hundred people serving this Temple. Think about it. Can a hundred be wrong because one man disagrees?'

'Yes,' said Hanno. 'I think they can.'

'You do, do you?' Dow looked thoughtful. 'Is that what you think? Go on.'

'The priest himself said that people are like sheep. They can be led.'

'He meant the people outside. Not those that Dwell in the Temple.'

'You are people, aren't you? And I am the Shepherd. I lead. Don't forget that, Dow. I am the Shepherd. The god chose me. Did he make a mistake, do you think?'

'The god cannot make a mistake. Your tongue should wither at the root.'

'Then I could well be right, couldn't I?'

'About what?'

Hanno opened his mouth and then closed it, slowly. He had forgotten what he was trying to prove in the effort of proving it. He began again, shakily. 'If I say that Aram spoke of worms and not of serpents; if I say that he never prophesied that I would bleed in the face, I could be right, couldn't I?'

'But you never said any of those things.'

Dow stepped back swiftly as Hanno's clawing hand harrowed the air where his neck would have been had he not moved. Hanno came after him.

'Never said? Never said? What do you mean, never said? You've taken my freedom away. Are you trying to take my memory too?'

'No one is –'

'The manuscript was altered. Did you think I wouldn't see that? You know now, don't you?'

'Know what? Shepherd, be calm.'

'If I saw no mark on Aram it was because I *couldn't* see it. Not because it wasn't there. You know that.'

'There was no mark.'

'But I couldn't tell. If he'd had a hole in his head I wouldn't have seen it in that light.'

'You see all you need to see.'

'And the manuscript?'

'What manuscript?'

'Dow, I warn you, I can see well enough if I know what to look for.'

'That's exactly what I said. You're becoming hysterical. You know what will happen,' said Dow. 'You'd better come into the garden anyway. You need fresh air. Come.'

The withered daisy chain still hung from the iron ring.

Aram would have liked that, thought Hanno. Dow lifted the end of the chain and looked at him.

Now you can't get away.

Hanno said aloud, 'After the Festival you can't hold me. My time will be up.'

'When you have testified.'

'Not otherwise?' Hanno looked up at the scaffolding.

'You surely weren't thinking of not testifying?'

'A Shepherd is always free to go home after the Festival.

The Book says so. How could you keep a Shepherd when his time was done?'

'But after the Festival you won't be Shepherd,' said Dow. 'You could be something else entirely. You might decide to retire to a cell, with a stool and a sand clock, and meditate for the rest of your life.'

Hanno leaned on the wall, afraid to leave its support although it heaved sickeningly under his shoulders.

'My father and brother might have something to say to that,' he said.

'I don't think so,' said Dow. 'Your father and brother are believers. Shall we go in?' He took a kerchief from his belt and gently dabbed the sweat from Hanno's eyes. 'And don't go bothering to look for the foot of that scaffolding,' he added. 'You haven't the strength to climb it.'

13

HE occupied his hours of confinement by turning the little sand clock at random intervals, and imagining that every time he did so the temple was flung violently into reverse, so that people were hurled back to the places they had occupied a few moments before. From memory he constructed an all-purpose worshipper. He put him through his paces; allowed him to walk in at the gate, purchase a serpent and cross the courtyard.

It takes one minute to get from the gate to the foot of the steps one two three four now you are buying your serpent eighteen nineteen twenty now you are passing the fountain, now you are crossing the gutter, mind you don't slip, twenty-eight twenty-nine thirty here is someone you don't much like, coming the other way, you would sooner not speak to him but one mustn't be churlish so close to the god forty-four forty-five now you'll have to slow down anyway because a queue is forming where people stop to hang up their serpents but never mind, you'll soon have one foot on the bottom step. See, I told you; fifty-nine, sixty!

Back you go.

He turned the clock and sent his wretched victim across the courtyard again. One day he thought, Suppose someone did this to me. I'd never get out: and in a panic he hurled the sand clock across the room. It hit the wall and shattered. When Dow came in he looked at the litter of glass and sand and at Hanno, crouched in the opposite corner with his knees drawn up under his chin.

'What happened?'

'I dropped it.'

'What a long arm you must have,' said Dow.

Nothing more was said about it, and the next morning they gave him another clock. He did not turn it. Time stopped.

One day he said, 'I should like to write a letter to my brother, if that's allowed?'

'Why shouldn't you write a letter to your brother?' said Dow.

'I have nothing to write with.' It was six months since he had written anything.

'Well, you know where the pens and ink are kept. There's plenty of paper.'

'But is it allowed?'

Dow looked, as he usually did these days, as though Hanno were wounding him to the heart with each word. He took his every protest personally.

'You speak as if we kept you a prisoner. It's for one hour a day, that's all. Anyone would think you were locked up all the time.'

'How long will it be before I am locked up all the time?' Hanno said. He went to the cabinet in the priest's quarters and fetched what he needed. On the way back he glanced towards the colonnade and saw that at some time during the day a table had been erected on the side of the sanctuary opposite his hut. A fine cloth, embossed with heavy embroidery, was draped over it. He went to look more closely and identified the design: an assembly of serpents tying themselves in knots about a garland of flowers, rose, lily, clover, woodbine, hemlock.

He sat down on his couch in the Hut and uncorked the jar of ink. He had the pen poised above the paper before the thought struck him: It's another altar. To Aram. Now they are going to worship him, too.

Ten minutes later he was still sitting there with the pen slipping from his fingers and a serpent of ink running down his arm. Egil and Dow came to fetch him.

'Shepherd. It's time.'

'Time for what?'

'You know. . .The Hour. . .It's time.'

He stared at them.

'No. But already, this morning. . .'

'No. You haven't. That was yesterday.'

'It was this morning. You know it was this morning. It was. It was.'

Dow leaned over him, desperately sympathetic. 'The Hour isn't in the morning. It never has been.'

'It was. Go away. I want to write my letter.'

'Don't be a fool,' said Egil, always the first to lose patience. 'You can bring your letter with you.'

The small window in the small room was very high up, but the walls were whitewashed. It was a bright small room. He put the paper and ink on the stool and sat on the floor. He could not actually see what he was writing, but the nib slid effortlessly over the paper.

Dear Ivo, it is only twelve days to the Festival and I shall be home again, but I cannot wait so long to see you. I wish you would come and see me. I am not well, I think. I wish you would come.

Dow stood at his elbow.

'The Hour is over. Have you finished your letter?' Hanno looked up and nodded, scattering pages. He seemed to have written rather a lot. 'Do you want me to deliver it for you?'

'Yes. If you would.'

Dow took the letter away. Hanno waited for several days, but Ivo did not visit him and he received no reply to his message. He came to the conclusion that Dow had never delivered it, but by this time he had come to the conclusion also that henceforth he was to be regularly locked up for two hours every day, while the worshippers fawned on the new altar and walked in and out of the open gate.

'Don't pretend any more,' he said wearily, to Egil. 'I can count up to two.'

'It always has been two,' said Egil. 'Right from the start.'

At least the food was still food. They did not give him ash and tell him it was porridge. This cheered him a little until he began to wonder if it really was ash, and he only thought it was porridge. He sat in the cookhouse at supper, stirring his soup and identifying the vegetables that floated to the surface.

Item: a bean. Item: a slice of carrot. Item: a scallion – out with it. Item: a lentil.

'Dow, what's this?'

Dow leaned across the table to look. 'A lentil.'

'That's what I thought. And this?'

'A pea.'

'Good. And this is a scallion?'

'Of course it is. What's the matter with you? There's nothing wrong with your eyes.'

Hanno smiled at him. 'Nor there is. But I thought you might tell me they were precious stones from the handle of the divine tooth-pick.'

Dow looked affronted at this product of Hanno's secret reserves of rudery. Hanno guessed that Dow thought he should have no secret reserves of anything, any more.

'Make the most of it,' said Egil. 'You'll get nothing after tomorrow night.'

'What do you mean?' He was cast down again, immediately. What were they planning to do with him now?

'The Shepherd fasts for a week before the Festival,' said Egil. 'You must have been told.'

Hearing this from Egil he was prepared to swear blind

that he had never been told anything of the kind, but after a few minutes of careful thought he recalled Dow describing what was in store for him, on the very day that he had been chosen. He had taken no notice, reckoning that he would worry about it when the time came. The time was on him, now.

'After tomorrow,' said Dow, 'there are no services. We Prepare ourselves for the Festival. The Temple is Closed.'

'Ha. No more Hours then?' said Hanno.

'Except for visits to the Shrine and the Altar of the Prophet,' said Egil. 'It's different this year. Everything's different this year. The people will have to be allowed to visit each day. There could be riots, otherwise,' he went on, happily.

'How many visits a day?' said Hanno. Losing all interest in the soup he pushed the bowl away from him.

'Three,' said Dow.

'As usual,' said Egil, experimentally.

Hanno put his elbows on the table and supported his head with his hands. By stiffening his fingers against his temples he was able to fix his eyes upon the two Guardians without wavering.

'You think I'm mad, don't you?' he said.

Dow, clad in his persona of the rejected friend, stopped eating, his spoon still in his mouth. Slowly, he removed the spoon. 'Not mad,' he said, pleadingly. 'How can you say that? But you must admit, you're not well.'

'I didn't say you'd driven me mad,' said Hanno, 'although that's not for want of trying.'

'You can't believe it.'

'But I'd have to be mad to believe anything you told me after what you've done. I'll grant you've succeeded up to a point. I don't know what's happening any more – but I know what *has* happened. You can't take my memory away. God knows what you've made of me, but I know what I was. I know what Aram was. He was a lunatic.

'He was no prophet. He spoke foolishness all his life, but he said one true thing. He said my nose bled. He *knew* that. He didn't prophesy, he saw me. You invented the rest.'

'He said he would die without a mark on him,' said Dow, 'and he did.'

'So you say.'

'You are mad,' said Egil. 'Everyone saw it.'

'Except me.'

'He said you feared death by water; can you deny that?' said Dow.

'Not any more. But he never said it.'

'He said you would be unwilling –'

'*You* said I would be unwilling –'

'– said you would be afraid of the dark.'

'I'm not afraid of the dark. Was that you in the slype, that day?'

'What day?'

'You lie to me, you lock me up – what have you done with my letter?'

Egil began to answer, 'But Shepherd, you haven't written –' Dow looked at him sharply. Hanno sensed a breakdown in communications.

'Do you remember what you said in your letter?' said Dow.

'More or less.' He was taken aback. No denials? No evasions?

'Oh yes, you still have your memory, don't you? Wait there.' Dow rose from the table and went out of the room. He returned a moment later with a sheet of paper – no, three sheets of paper. 'This is your letter. I couldn't deliver it.'

Hanno took up the sheets and began to read, painfully, the dislocated hand that he barely knew as his own.

Dear Ivo, it is only twelve days to the Festival and I shall be home again, but I cannot wait so long to see you. I wish *you would come and see me. I am not well, I think. I wish you would come. Does do you do do you remember I told you I think i don't understand what has happened that they tell me things i dont remember do you tell you dear Ivo come and see me I wish you would come and Dear ivo come and see me PLEASE ivo come and see me...*The writing grew larger towards the foot of the page until there were only three or four words to the line. *IVO COME AND SEE ME.* He turned to the next sheet, and the third. *IVO COME AND SEE ME IVO COME AND SEE ME IVO COME AND SEE ME IVO IVO IVO IVO IVO IVO...*

'I couldn't, could I?' said Dow. 'Would you really want anyone to see that?'

Hanno looked down at the table-top, seeing the green river and the elder-flowers and whispered, 'My brother loves me. He would have come.'

'Just so,' said Egil.

'He loves the god too,' said Dow, pityingly. 'You should know better than to divide his loyalty. Anyway,' he said, suddenly jolly. 'You'll see him again in a week.'

'Unless?' said Hanno.

'Unless.'

'I won't do it,' he said. 'I won't do your lying for you.'

Nothing happened. They left him sitting at the table and went away.

When the gate had closed upon the last worshipper, after the last service before the Festival, the flotilla of ladies made a final sally across the temple with their mops, eddying round the sanctuary, pausing to bob in front of the altar of the Prophet. Then they too went back to the city and left the Dwellers in the Temple to get down to the serious business of preparing for the celebrations. The Guardians left their posts and with their off-duty companions retired to their hall to contemplate. The Handmaidens withdrew to their hall to contemplate. Even the acolyte disappeared. The altar was stripped of its vessels and in their place lay the vestments of the Shepherd, the belt, the sheepskin and the head-dress, absorbing virtue and awaiting the day when the Shepherd should put them on for the last time.

Hanno was hauled off to an unknown room and presented with new clothes to try on. When he was decently covered a little woman came in and danced round him with pins and tapes. At first he took this to be the preliminaries to another rite, but she turned out to be a seamstress, come to see if the clothes fitted.

'They fit perfectly,' he assured her, gravely, touched by her artless pride in the workmanship. 'How did you guess the size?'

'We measured them against your own,' she said. 'Is not this too tight? And here?'

'A perfect fit,' he said again. 'What are they for?'

'For the Festival. The Shepherd must have new Garments for the Festival.'

She seemed a sane little woman, absorbed in her craft, but she wore a serpent at her shoulder. Through the window Hanno could see another leg of the scaffolding, but the window was a mere slash in the stonework, and there was no door.

It was the hour of the evening service; there was no evening service. Hanno left the sewing room and walked for a while in the garden, craning his neck and trying to calculate where the other two legs of the scaffold came to earth; in the maze of little courtyards between the temple and the wall. If he could find them he could climb them, whatever Dow might think. The gardener came to lock the gate and Hanno wandered back to the sanctuary and watched the courtyard turn pink, then red, as the sun fell westwards behind the temple, sending the domed shadow crawling up the wall. A little reflected light glowed on the new altar and Hanno saw a number of worms, serpents since their promotion, basking in the late warmth. They were no longer the business of the god: in future Aram would take care of his own.

The courtyard grew darker. He could not see the guards at the gate; they became one with their shadows and vanished. A single red star came up over the rim of the wall, mirrored by the single red star above the altar that was the sanctuary lamp. The voice of the city diminished until the only sound that he could hear was the subdued chanting, low and unmusical, from the hall of the Guardians.

He was invisible. No one knew that he sat there. Now is the moment to disappear, he thought. Now to find a hiding-place in the night. But if he hid they would find him by daylight and drag him out. He could imagine only too well what they might do to him after that, and he chose to think of other things. Ivo; the river; the boat. The elder-flowers. In a week it would all be given back to him if he would only do what they wanted him to do.

I can't do it.

I must find the scaffolding. Why did I wait so long?

He knew already that he had waited too long, but the darkness was entire and he was at home in it. Leaving the Hut, he stepped over the sanctuary railing and, beginning with the slype, visited every door in the long row that ended with the entry to the priest's quarters. Each was locked, except for the first. If he went out and drowned himself no one would object, only they knew that this was the one thing he would never do. And if you go now, he told himself, you cannot go home.

As he made his way back to the sanctuary gate, the temple bell rang once, in the dome, scattering bats. At any other time this would have been the signal for sleep, but he remembered the ritual. This time was like no other. He turned and found the path that led to the door of the Guardians' hall, sorrel, clover, mallow, lily, spurge, a smooth stone, as cold as water, where he stood and rapped three times on the door, with his staff. The door was opened less than an inch, and strung a warp of light from sill to lintel. He saw no one, but a voice asked,

'Who knocks?'

'The Shepherd knocks.'

'What does the Shepherd seek?'

The voice was Frey's. Hanno longed to say, Look, Frey, let us stop arsing about. You know perfectly well why I am here. He replied,

'The Shepherd seeks a companion to share his vigil.' He didn't want a companion. Darkness had hitherto been his guarantee of solitude, but the Book decreed that during the time of his fast he should choose a companion to watch with him until dawn; ostensibly to reinforce his prayers but, more probably, he thought, to make sure that he ate nothing.

'Who does the Shepherd choose, this night?'

'You'd do,' said Hanno, accommodatingly.

'You're not meant to say that,' Frey said, in a fury. 'You know I can't leave here. I'm the Door Keeper, tonight.'

'The Shepherd chooses Arlo.' He named someone he scarcely knew.

'Return to your Hut, Shepherd, and he that you seek shall be sent after you.' The door closed, leaving him in the dark. He moved away, sorrel, windflower, woodbine... Woodbine? He had missed the path. He took one step backwards and found it again, spurge, rose, clover...It crossed his mind that he might go for a walk, leaving Arlo to find the Hut empty. He could cross and encircle the temple by a score of routes, from flower to flower, bypassing obstacles and making detours. In the dark they might search for him for hours. In his mind he saw the place alive with silently tiptoeing figures, arms groping unsuccessfully.

No one would be even slightly amused.

He returned to the Hut, the red eye of the sanctuary lamp ever in view. That could see him, always.

He was supposed to be praying. When Arlo arrived, some minutes later, he found the Shepherd prostrated in fervent devotion on the floor of his Hut. The companion was meant to stand outside the Hut, so that the Shepherd's attention might not be diverted, but after listening for a while to the increasingly regular breathing, he stepped inside and touched him ungently in the side, with his foot.

'Kneel, Shepherd.'

Hanno raised his head, half-asleep, which was more or less what Arlo had expected.

'What do you want?'

'It may fool the Priest, but it doesn't fool us,' said Arlo. 'You are required to spend your nights in prayer. Pray.'

Hanno struggled to his knees at once. By his voice he knew that the Guardian was not feeling playful.

'What makes you think I wasn't praying?' he asked, sullenly.

'We don't think – we know,' said Arlo. 'You've been getting away with it long enough; but there are six days left. Pray,' he said. 'And think about the Festival.'

Hanno thought about the Festival.

He was still thinking about the Festival when Arlo left him at sunrise. He thought about himself, in the belt and the sheepskin and the head-dress, standing before the multitude and bleating his ludicrous testimony to the miraculous death of the Prophet. He thought more urgently about the small room with the small window, and wondered how well he would come to know it. He thought of Ivo, believing without question everything that he was told, except for the things that his brother told him. Truth was so much sand. Turn the clock and tell it another way. No two grains ever fall together a second time. Every time that man crosses the courtyard, something changes. Every time they speak, something changes. The sand will run and run on that day. He threw himself on to the couch, and fell asleep.

It was fully day when he woke. Dow stood by the couch, and a remote thudding in his head made him put his hand to his nose, fearfully, until he realized that the thumping came from elsewhere.

'They are knocking at the gate, to be let in,' said Dow. 'Hurry up. It isn't seemly to keep the faithful waiting.'

Hanno said, 'You believe in obedience to the Book, don't you Dow? You above anyone. Doesn't it offend you to see the rituals broken?'

'These are strange times,' said Dow, looking as if he suspected that this devious person was trying to entrap him.

'What does the Book say about Strange Times?'

'You never cared what the Book said before.'

'The Shepherd needs to know nothing,' said Hanno. 'I know nothing. And in any case, I can hardly see to read, as you very well know.'

'I don't know that,' said Dow, automatically. 'Why seek knowledge now?'

Hanno shrugged. He was finding it very difficult to concentrate. 'I just wondered – for so long everything is done as the Book says it must be done. Now, suddenly, things are different.'

'I think you should see the Book,' said Dow. 'I'll speak to the Priest. Now, hurry. The people are waiting.'

'Don't. Not on my account,' said Hanno.

'I'll speak to the Priest.' Dow produced his keys and opened the door of the small room.

'How long shall I be in here?'

'An hour, as usual.'

'I thought three.'

'One hour now, one at noon, and one before evening,' said Dow, closing the door on the last of his recital.

At noon they approached the door of the small room and went straight past it.

'Where?'

'In here.' Dow conjured again with keys and opened another door, further along the passage. Hanno, looking over his shoulder, saw a stout post in the middle of the floor, and a dangling loop of chain.

'Why?' He thought the chain was for him, but Dow nudged him round to the other side of the post. It supported a lectern and on the lectern was a book. The book was the prisoner, bound in brass.

'I spoke to the Priest,' said Dow. 'And he agrees with me. We think you should read this.'

'A book?'

'The Book.'

'Oh.' It *was* a book. He had imagined letters of fire, alive in the air.

'Read it.'

'I don't know that I can.'

'At all events,' said Dow, 'look at it. Carefully.'

The door, like all the others, closed and was locked. Hanno prowled unsteadily round the lectern, measuring the length of the chain. There was enough slack to reach the ground, so he lowered the Book to the floor and sat cross-legged before it, head well down; too dizzy to stay on his feet.

He skipped through the Rite of the Guard and the Rite of the Guardians; the Rite of the Shepherd, which he knew, and the Rite of the Bowl which had nothing to do with him.

The Rite of the Daily Service was followed by the Rite of the Handmaidens, which surprised him. At last he found what he was looking for: the Rite of the Great Festival at the Year's Turn, and the Rite of the Days before the Festival.

On the Evening of the Seventh Day before the Festival, the Gate of the Temple shall be shut and barred with Strong Bars, and it shall remain so for Seven Days, and none shall go out and none shall go in.

And the people without the Gate shall make themselves ready to enter the Temple on the Seventh Day after the Closing of the Gate, and the people within the Gate, they that are Dwellers in the Temple, shall make ready to receive those that are without the Gate.

The ancient scribe who had put this law into words had cared nothing for brevity. He had been concerned only with making himself clear. He had succeeded.

Hanno found him very clear indeed. The gate must be shut and no one must pass in or out. Voices came to him through the door. At this moment the gate was open, and people were passing in from the city, and would shortly pass out again. The ritual was broken. The words were as negligible as a child's scribble on a paving stone. They meant nothing. He turned back to the Rite of the Shepherd.

On the Day of the Festival, when the Shepherd has stood before the people for the last time, he shall go out of the Gate and be seen no more in the Temple, and he shall be no more the Shepherd. And the Next Day shall be performed the Rite of the Choosing.

He knew about the Rite of the Choosing. That was not his problem any longer. He read again:

. . .he shall go out of the Gate. . .and he shall be no more the Shepherd.

The Rite of the Days was broken. The Rite of the Festival was going to be broken, and he was going to break it, with his testimony. So who cared if the Rite of the Shepherd were broken? Who would protest if the Shepherd did not walk out of the gate and be no more the Shepherd?

His father? Ivo? They might inquire, diffidently, when their Hanno would be home.

Oh, my sons, says the priest, all that is changed. We are living in Strange Times. We have appointed him Perpetual Shepherd.

Oh, says Father, a little upset. Shan't we see him again?

Of course you will see him again, says the priest. Once a year we'll let him out on a string and he can visit you for five whole minutes.

That's all right, then, says Father, and trots home again.

Or:

Oh, my sons, says the priest, all that is changed. We are living in Strange Times.

But you have just chosen another Shepherd, says Ivo. Where's my little brother?

He decided to devote the remainder of his days to the service of the god, says the priest. He begged us to wall him up in a small room with a small window and a small stool and a small sand clock and at his most earnest request we nailed his feet to the floor.

How wonderful, says Ivo. Now Father can die happy.

Anise?

I had a lover once, says Anise, but they took him away and he never came back. There are plenty of others.

Something dropped on to the page. Hanno rocked back on his heels, alarmed and afraid to look, one hand over his eyes and the other over his nose. Nothing else seemed to be happening so he removed his hands and peered at the Book. It was a tear that had fallen there, first magnifying the word *Shepherd* and now dissolving it. Wretchedly ashamed, he blotted at the page with the hem of his tunic, and blamed his over-stressed eyes for failing him. The writing was not too badly disfigured, but as he examined it he noticed that the ink, although aged and faded, was very similar to the kind used by the priest. Had he made a real mess of it, all a scribe need do would be to lift the remaining letters and write the word again. He looked more closely, holding his head sideways and squinting across the bridge of his nose. Someone had lifted some letters and written a word again. More than that; the page had been rewritten.

The entire Rite of the Shepherd had been rewritten.

His hands began to shake, tugging the leaves against the thread that anchored them. He fumbled through the pages until he came again to the Rite of the Festival. That too had been altered at length. It had been altered how many years, how many hundreds of years ago? And how many times? Things were not as they had been. The ritual was as pliable as a withy; as plastic as clay. They could make of it what they wanted. They could make of him what they wanted.

Oh no, he said. He wailed, No no no no no, and rocked backwards and forwards over his folded arms like the desolate child he had always been, while the tears ran into his mouth, unchecked.

14

INTO the small room and out of the small room, into the Hut, the daylight and the dark. To the door of the Guardians' hall, What does the Shepherd seek? The Shepherd seeks a companion to share his vigil. Who does the Shepherd choose this night, back to the Hut, sorrel, windflower, spurge, rose, clover. He never asked for Dow or Egil.

Every day Dow took him to the small room, three times there and three times back. When Hanno went to the bath house Dow went with him and swam up and down, three strokes this way, three strokes that. Dow brought him water to the Hut. It was all he was allowed until the Festival.

'Then you'll be home again, eating what you like,' said Dow.

Oh yes?

He was no longer hungry. The fierce consuming fire in his chest that had burned him so in the first days of his fast, now only smouldered a little. Whether in the Hut or in the small room he lay down, either on the couch or on the floor, and sometimes slept and sometimes did not. Half-sleeping he followed Dow to and from the room, to and from the Hut, admitting the truth of the priest's prediction that when the Shepherd went he went consenting. Wherever the Shepherd went he went consenting; that much was assured. He was too weak to do anything but consent; he thought sometimes that it was not fasting that had weakened him.

One night the chosen companion was less vigilant than

his predecessors. Hanno fell asleep, praying (Why am I here? What am I for? What shall I do?) propped against the couch, and remained undetected until morning. Consequently he was more alert than usual when Dow came to fetch him. He became aware of the picture he must present, plodding like a sheep at the heels of a shepherd.

I'm the Shepherd.

Oh yes?

Dow led him as surely as if there were a string round his neck. If there really had been a string round his neck his position would have been no more undignified than it was now. It was a day for decisions; time to stop consenting. When Dow opened the door and stood back to let him enter, he froze against the wall in the cool passage and would not move. This was not precisely a decision.

'Go in,' said Dow.

'No,' said Hanno. 'Enough. Not today.'

'Go in.' Dow put out his hand, to shove. Hanno put out his hand, on the end of his long arm, to close it around Dow's throat, and Dow, all armed with the Knowledge that Makes a Small Man Great, plucked the hand away and the small man threw Hanno across the room, just as Hanno had thrown the sand clock. Then he locked the door. When it was time to open it again neither of them mentioned the incident.

'Feeling better?' was all Dow said, cheerfully, as though Hanno had been a little indisposed. Hanno was sitting against the wall where he had landed. He had been thinking. It was a day for decisions.

'Come on,' said Dow, genially impatient. 'You don't want to spend the rest of the day in here?'

'No.'

'It's the last day.'

Hanno didn't believe him. He had forgotten that there was going to be a last day.

'Tomorrow is the Festival.'

Definitely a day for decisions. He stood up.

'Dow?'

'Shepherd?'

'Did you know that the Book of the Ritual had been altered?'

Dow ushered him out. 'Of course. It's hardly a secret.'

Of course. That's why you showed me.

'No one told me,' said Hanno.

'You didn't ask. Anyone would have told you, only you never seemed very interested. Unwilling,' he said, teasingly. 'You haven't been upsetting yourself about it? Have you? Is *that* why you were crying?'

'Why has it been altered?'

'Because the Rites have changed. People used to be less enlightened in the old days. They used to sacrifice – a sheep, I dare say – at the altar. One wouldn't do that now.'

'The tapestry,' said Hanno.

'What tapestry?'

'The one Aram – the prophet – used as a tent-cloth. It shows a ram being sacrificed.'

'Oh, that. I'm surprised you could see what it shows,' said Dow. Hanno's blurred eyes sought his, reproachfully. 'It's very worn,' he amended, hurriedly.

Never admit...

'Was it worrying you?'

'It didn't worry me, but I never liked it.'

'There you are, then. Nobody liked it. That's why the Ritual was changed.'

They reached the Hut. Hanno went in and sat down on the couch. The Ritual was not an evil trick after all. The Ritual was Good. It changed for the better. It did not devour its victims.

Dow stood by the doorway. 'Probably some Prophet arose and revealed to the people that the sacrifice was not pleasing to the god, and so it was stopped. Now another Prophet has arisen. And you will testify to his Miraculous Death.'

Hanno turned and looked at the figure outlined in the doorway, his gratitude all at once overpowered by suspicion.

'You will testify to his Miraculous Death?'

'No.'

'My son,' said the priest. 'What will the people do if their Shepherd fails them?

'Tomorrow they will come to the Festival, full of joy, to hear the Shepherd tell how the Prophet was found Dead, without a mark on him. They believe, they bring their offerings, they sing with loud voices, and yet the Shepherd is silent. What will they think?

'They will think they have been deceived. All along they have known that it was the Shepherd who found the Prophet. No one can speak for the Shepherd, he must speak for himself; and if he will not, what will the people believe?

'My son, you must tell them what they want to hear.'

'No.'

They beseeched him. To the small room and back again, pale pleading faces, by columns and arches, in the Hut and out of it; Cariola and Nola, Arlo, Frey, Dow, Egil, contemptuous but persuading as hard as the rest.

'Shepherd –'

'No.'

'The Prophet –'

'No.'

'The Miracle –'

'No. I don't believe in your prophet or your miracle.'

'Shepherd –'

'No.'

He refused to get up. Instead he lay there and looked at them. I don't believe in your prophet or your miracle or your god. He closed his eyes upon the crescent of misty moons that hung featureless above him. At last it began to grow dark and they left him alone. He remained on the couch without moving until the bell roused him. For the last time he trod the path to the Guardians' door, stood on the stone as cold as water and rapped three times with his staff. For the last time the door opened.

'Who knocks?'

Hanno leaned his head against the door jamb.

'The Shepherd knocks.'

'What does the Shepherd seek?'

'The Shepherd seeks a companion to share his vigil.'

'Who does the Shepherd choose, this night?'

'The fellow whose eyebrows meet in the middle – I can't remember his name.'

There was an angry hiss on the other side of the door and it slammed as well as it could with only an inch to go.

Hanno started back towards the sanctuary, sorrel, windflower, spurge, rose, clover. . .He knelt down in the Hut, conveniently close to the couch, so that with luck he might sleep as he had slept last night, and waited for his companion. No one came. He went to the doorway and listened. There was no sound of boot or sandal approaching the sanctuary, no unshod foot crossing the tiles towards the Hut. Perhaps he had so offended the fellow with the eyebrows that met in the middle that he refused to come. Perhaps the door keeper had been the fellow with the eyebrows that met in the middle. Whatever the reason, no one came.

He arose and left the Hut. On his right the sanctuary lamp hung unwavering. There was no wind. The air was heavy with rain and the sky outside the temple as dark as the domed roof within. He walked towards the unguarded colonnade and stood leaning against a pillar. It was a warm night. He could smell white flowers. He thought of the elder tree, the river and the boat, and all the things that might be his again tomorrow if he chose to earn them. He thought he heard a sound in the temple. Perhaps his companion had arrived after all, and was already searching for him. Very reluctantly he turned and went in again. The sound was not repeated.

Inside he found that it was darker than ever after the faint relief of the open night. He could make out nothing but the sanctuary lamp, guttering smokily now as if the air were disturbed around it. He mounted the steps and found the first tile of his path back to the Hut. The lamp was before him, a little to his left, rose, lily, mallow, clover, rose, spurge, rose –

The lamp went out.

He stopped where he stood and stared at the place where the lamp had been.

How could it go out, unless. . .There was a small sound and for an instant he saw the lamp again. He knew then that it had never gone out. Someone had stood between him and the light; someone was beside him and behind him. He put out his arms to ward off the encroaching presence, opened his mouth to protest, and got no further. As he tried to turn, unseen hands caught his unseen arms and pulled him forward until he fell to his knees and someone, it seemed, was kneeling across his ankles. He thought he had been seized by a creature with an indefinite number of arms and legs. He was pinned in a paralysed arc with someone's knee in the small of his back, someone's fingers laced into his hair and tugging at his head, a hand pressed over his mouth, forcing it shut, and more hands fastened along the length of his outstretched arms.

All done in the dark. How had they found him? Who were they? Where the sanctuary lamp had been a dull yellow light shone out from a shuttered lantern. It was directed at his own face, but a little of the light fell on the person who held the lantern.

Dow.

'Oh, it's you,' said Dow. 'We thought it was some fool who didn't know the Ways of the Temple.' He thought that having recognized him they would release him, but the hands gripped more tightly and the fingers in his hair pulled his head back still further. '*You* know the Ways of the Temple, don't you?'

It was clear that no one expected him to answer. He turned his eyes upward and in the pale light saw Egil's inverted face grinning down at him. He should have known. Only Egil was tall enough to come between him and the light.

Dow brought the lantern closer. 'You can't move, can you?'

He tried to shake his head, but Egil only clasped it more firmly, as though it were a trophy, already severed.

'You can't speak?'

This time Egil shook his head for him, using his jaw as a handle, and he felt his teeth sink into his lip.

'You could die like this; unheard.'

Dow advanced his hand and something caught the light. Hanno scarcely had time to decide what it might be before he felt a coldness at his throat.

'Unseen.'

Dow himself vanished into the dark as he raised the lantern with one hand and pressed the knife down tenderly with the other. Hanno knew without seeing that he had drawn blood, and his heart set up a dreadful, slow slamming against his racked chest.

'Like a sheep,' said Dow, in the darkness. 'But that is no longer the Way of the Ritual, is it? There are other Ways.'

The light found him again as he sheathed the knife at his

belt, leaving his killing hand empty. He slowly crooked the fingers until his whole hand made a rigid claw; the pincers towards Hanno's fascinated eyes. 'Yes, you can see this, can't you?' Still slowly he brought it down until it rested where the knife had rested, squeezed gently and said incautious with conceit,

'The Knowledge that Makes a Small Man Great. Who would know?'

There would be no mark on me. Hanno was very glad that he couldn't open his mouth, for he would certainly have cried out, '*Aram.* So that's how –' He made no sign at all that he had understood anything. Dow raised the lantern again and surveyed him carefully.

'Do you remember what I once said? Think what a dozen of us could do? We will do it, Shepherd, if we must.' He slammed down the shutter and the light was hidden.

'Let him go.'

They let him go, all at once, so that he dropped where he knelt. He pressed himself against the floor and in the darkness felt them move away.

When at last he looked up, the darkness was absolute. He could not see the sanctuary lamp. On hands and knees he cast about, wildly spreading the tiles with his palms, aconite, poppy, arum, hemlock, nightshade. . .they had dragged him god knew where, off course. He was lost; darkness all round him, below, above. He extended his hands in front of him and one of them struck a pillar. He was beside a pillar. Clutching at it he began to edge round, crouching. The red lamp above the altar hung before him again, a little to his left. Still crouching he hauled himself across the tiles, strange flowers, and into the Hut. Still crouching he backed up against the couch and leaned on its safe solidity, staring out into the treacherous night. The last prophecy had come true.

He was afraid of the dark.

*

Still crouching, an hour later, he heard rain falling. The black pressure of the clouds was relieved as the water came down, purling in the steep gutters overhead. The air turned cooler. A little surge of wind set the sanctuary lamp swinging and in response another light sprang up on the far side of the colonnade. Hanno watched it draw near to the Hut, held high in a steady hand.

Again.

As he knelt against the couch his head had fallen back and he felt his throat exposed to the light held high in the steady hand, and to anything else that might be held in the other hand, which would be no less steady. He instantly bowed his head and battened his fingers over the back of his neck.

Dow stopped in the doorway and looked down at him.

'The Oblate discovered in an Attitude of Prayer,' he said, as if describing a picture. 'Attitude being the operative word. It would be too much to hope that you really are praying?'

Hanno looked up sideways to say 'No', but managed only a soundless grimace; his voice had abandoned him. He tried again: 'What have you come for?' Still no sound. Dow stood the lantern on the table.

'I didn't really imagine you were,' he said. 'It's a pity we didn't find out sooner; we might have expected less of you. Don't look so frightened,' he said. 'I've come to share your Vigil.'

Hanno found his voice at last. 'I didn't choose you.'

'I chose you,' said Dow. 'I think that tonight your Companion should be someone who understands you. Arlo, for instance, thought he could make you pray. I know better than that. You may be on your knees but you surely aren't praying. Why don't you sleep?' He reached across the table and picked up the folded blanket that lay on the couch. Hanno watched him lift the blanket and hold it out, draped over his upturned hands. 'Lie down and sleep. It's forbidden, of course, but that won't make any difference to you, will it? I won't tell anyone.'

Hanno could think only of suffocation. If Dow were to fall on him now and wrap the blanket round his face, stifling his screams, then his lungs, then his life, he would have no strength to resist or fight him off. And there would be no mark on him.

'Now lie down,' said Dow.

Hanno dared not answer in case he betrayed himself with a terrified whoop when he tried to draw breath. To his horror he found that he was crawling, forwards, sideways, out of the Hut, into the dark. He wanted to stand up and run, but it was no longer possible to stand up in the dark. His quivering arms gave way and pitched him headlong among roses. Dow came after him in three strides, caught him up by the shoulders and heaved him back to the couch.

'I told you to go to sleep.' His voice was angry, and not a little shaken. 'Now, go to sleep, or by god I'll give you such a clout you won't wake up for a week.'

Hanno turned his face to the hurdles, then rolled over in a fright because his back was to the darkness, and unprotected.

'Lie still, damn you. Go to sleep.'

Convinced that he would not sleep he lay still, and closed his eyes against the night. After a little while he began to dream of elder-flowers, drifting idly on deep water. He knew it was a dream because he could see so clearly.

He woke in the morning and Dow had gone. In his place stood the acolyte and in his arms were the vestments of the Shepherd.

'The sun has risen,' he said, in the voice of one announcing an unfortunate accident. 'Arise also and put on your Garments, Shepherd.'

Hanno gaped at him, but his mouth was bruised and yawning hurt. The sun was still low and the acolyte was a fiery apparition in the doorway of the Hut. Birds sang. The silence of the last seven days had evaporated with the rain and laughter echoed round the colonnade. The apparition tapped its foot.

'Arise also and put on your Garments, Shepherd.'

'In here?'

'No, not in here,' the acolyte snapped. 'In the Robing Room as usual. I've been waiting half an hour already.' He stalked off, the belt clanking dismally against his knee as he walked. Hanno sat up and looked to the end of the couch. Someone, presumably Dow, had thrown the blanket over him during the night, and he was still wearing the clothes he had fallen asleep in. He was fairly sure that he had been wearing them for the past week, and got out of bed to find clean ones before going to the bath house.

The temple turned like a water wheel. He caught hold of the table and it receded from his touch. The floor began to pour out of the doorway, flowing so swiftly that he could not distinguish one tile from another. A clot of sunlight fell from the wall and spread.

Stooping very carefully, he lowered himself to the ground, hoping that it would take his weight. It shifted a little, and then settled under him, although for some moments longer ripples rolled out towards the sanctuary rail. At random he raked up an armful of clothes and then, clinging to his staff like a punt pole, edged out of the Hut and made his way to the slype.

The acolyte's head appeared round the door of the Robing Room. 'Hurry up!'

The slype was dark and close. He tried to hurry through it, thinking of the fingers in his hair and the knife at his throat, but he reached the far door and he was still alive. The water lay at his feet. He looked down into it, and stepped back quickly as it surged up in a gigantic bubble, and broke, and was sucked back into a bottomless trough.

He undressed and slid into the water before it could move again. It was cold and the shock revived him a little, so that he was able to climb out before any waiting hand could clasp his ankle and draw him down for ever.

The ledge round the cistern began to rock gently and he sat down on a bench to put on his clothes. At first he thought he had made a mistake and brought someone else's garments. Everything seemed too large. He supposed that they had been put in the Hut by the acolyte and were the required outfit for a Shepherd at the Festival. The trousers were of a far superior quality to anything he normally wore, and they were gartered with leather thongs instead of the usual cloth strips. The tunic was white, with very full sleeves that were caught in at the wrist. He put that on too and as he belted it he remembered that he had worn these clothes before. He remembered the little seamstress with her tapes and pins and her shy pride; and he remembered telling her that she was right to be proud because the clothes fitted perfectly. They did not fit now.

He took the staff in hand again and set off on the journey to the Robing Room. As he opened the door of the slype someone opened the door of the cookhouse and the heavy smell of frying fish rolled out. Cariola rolled out.

'Hurry up,' said the acolyte, kicking the wall in his impatience. It seemed that he had been there, with his head round the door, all the time. He peered offensively into Hanno's face. 'What are you doing?'

'Shepherd!' Cariola was on him, like a great muslin bag full of rose petals. 'Whatever's the matter?' The miasma of fried fish overpowered him and he leaned on the staff, retching miserably, unable to make the last few paces to the Robing Room and safety.

'Now what's he done?' Dow came up from somewhere, a governess again, weighed down by little cares.

'*He's* not going to give us much trouble,' said Egil, close by, sounding unusually pleased with himself.

Hanno was inclined to agree. A hand took the staff from his hand, and another led him into the Robing Room. The acolyte, praying monotonously like a defective hurdy-gurdy, pulled the sheepskin jerkin over his head and wound the belt round his waist. He paused in mid-prayer and said, 'You've lost weight.'

'He's been fasting,' said Egil, at his shoulder.

'No one ever got that thin through a week's fasting,' said the acolyte, fretfully, as though the lost weight were temple property and had to be accounted for. 'What have you been doing to him?' He raised his eyebrows at Egil who smiled at him and shrugged. The acolyte smiled too.

He lifted the head-dress and pulled it down over Hanno's ears. 'Your hair's still wet,' he complained. 'You wear it too long.'

'Oh, no,' said Egil, 'it's a very useful length.' He tugged at a lock that had strayed from under the head-dress. 'Something to get hold of. Eh?'

'Go now to the Altar, Shepherd,' said the acolyte, suddenly formal again. 'Go in peace before the god, for the last time, and come no more to this place.' He held the door open and as Hanno stepped outside, he handed him the staff. In the space of the Robing Rite it had been wreathed in flowers, rose, lily, mallow, elder.

Elder, river, boat.

He walked to the sanctuary, one hand on the staff, one hand on the railing, and set his feet on the path to the altar, rose, lily, mallow, clover, rose. Since the removal of the vestments by the acolyte, the altar vessels had been replaced. Aram's favourite, the portly vase with the slender neck, had been removed altogether. Now it stood on the altar of the Prophet, surrounded by serpents. In its place was a new bowl that Aram would have admired even more, for it shone. It was made of silver and it was big enough to bathe a baby in.

At either side curved handles depended from knops of flowers too minutely wrought for Hanno's eyes. A manifestation of increased revenues, it stood like a fat and prosperous relative among the humbler relicts of the old regime. Hanno saw reflections slither in it and turned his face away. He knelt before the altar, laid his staff beside him, and raised his head, eyes closed, in the attitude of prayer.

Why am I here?

I am here to serve the god in the name of the people.

And?

I am here to testify to the Miraculous Death of the Prophet who was found by me, on the Day of the Serpent, with No Mark on him.

You are going to say that, are you?

It is the will of the people. I am the servant of the god in the name of the people. I am the Ritual Shepherd.

Are you?

He opened his eyes and found that he was staring straight at the underside of the silver bowl. He was looking at a grotesque image of himself, reflected in the shining surface, and he was close enough to know the truth of what he saw: a long, pallid face, long curved nose, deeply cloven upper lip, large frightened eyes that threatened to change places in the middle; high shoulders clad in white fleece and a great coiled horn on either side.

Not the Ritual Shepherd but the Ritual Sheep.

He shut his eyes for a second and then looked again. Haaaanno.

Why am I here? Oh god, why am I here?

He started up, his weakness forgotten. Behind him the

gate was open, and the worshippers were crowding in to the courtyard, wonderfully dressed for the crowning of the year. The Guardians stood at their places under the colonnade; no one was off-duty today. The Handmaidens waited on the steps with their arms filled with flowers, and at the gate of the sanctuary stood the priest distributing blessings with both hands, like a drunken merchant chucking away his surplus profits. Nobody was watching Hanno. Steadying himself against the altar he moved round to the back, where the Cell of the Prophet, uncurtained in honour of the day, stood banked with garlands and glowing interiorly with perfumed lamps. Hanno eased himself past it, out of the light, into the musty shadows where the aged eye, without intelligence, still looked out at him. He pulled the tapestry clear of the broken hurdles and brought it back to the front of the Cell, where he spread it out on the tiles in the full light of the lamps. Now even he could see it.

There stood the man with the knife, one hand raised, one hand wound into the wool at the back of the animal's neck. And there was the animal, forced down on its haunches, its head dragged back against its fleecy shoulders, and a chain about its body, staring at death with its one despairing eye. It was not a sheep, awaiting the knife: it was a man, in a sheepskin jerkin, and a belt of bronze links, and a horned head-dress.

Oh Dow, said Hanno. The Ritual has changed. The Ritual has changed. It has changed indeed.

15

PEOPLE were less enlightened in the old days.

No. No. Nothing has changed. They must still have their human sacrifice.

Aram, I will not testify that you were found dead without a mark on you. You were the sacrifice.

What will I say? Oh god, what shall I say? If I say nothing they will have me too. If they hadn't needed their witness they would have done it last night. They will kill me or keep me here for ever. There is no miracle. There is no prophet. There is no god, oh god what shall I do?

On the other side of the altar, beyond the sanctuary rail, the well of the temple was full. Hanno had never seen it so full in all his life. The crowd swayed and sang. Ecstatic chants rose here and there, flowers were thrown, jewelled serpents gleamed in triumph. The priest stood in the middle of the sanctuary, waiting for the sun to reach a certain window in the clerestory and shine down on him, so that the Festival might begin.

What happens if the sun doesn't shine? Hanno thought irrelevantly, as he walked round the altar again. I can't remember a Festival when the sun didn't shine, but it must happen sometimes. He stooped by the altar to pick up his staff, and approached the priest from behind. I could beat the old devil to death with this. He must have known what happened, whatever they told him, but his temple is full and his prophet is worshipped, so damn the truth. All that matters is the temple. He looked over his shoulder and addressed the god. Look out, god. If you're not careful they'll forget about you altogether. They'll write you out of the ritual and then where will you be? Flakes of soot, god. Flakes of soot.

The sanctuary lamp, almost extinguished by the brilliance of the sunshine, flickered.

I hope you're paying attention, god. This is me, Hanno; remember? Your Shepherd. You chose me out of dozens. I didn't believe in you but I did my best for you and look where it got me. You can do something for me, now. Tell me what to say.

And then find me a way out.

And if you cannot do that, then let me die fighting and never consent.

A movement caught his attention. Beyond the rail of the sanctuary a door was opened. It was the door to the Guardians' hall. Some belated Guardian, on his way to his post in the colonnade, hurried out and left the door swinging. Hanno saw into the hall for the first time. He screwed his eyes into slits and stared. At the other end of the hall was a second door, also open. It gave on to a small sunny courtyard, and in the middle of the courtyard a wooden pylon went up and out of sight. It was the scaffolding.

Ah, said Hanno. Thank you, god. Shall I go now?

No. Everyone is watching, and anyway, we have something to do first, don't we, god? That is, I have something to do, if you can think what it is. I can't think any more. Don't expect it.

The garland of sunlight that crept across the tiles rose lily sorrel aconite reached the priest at last, and the great Rite of the Festival of the Year's Turn began.

At some unseen signal the seething crowd fell quiet, and in the thick air the anguished moan of the bagpipe rose and fell. The flute keened mournfully in approximate harmony. Hanno felt his teeth go on edge as the fiddle swam up to join them, and the little tabor stuttered and spat all along.

Those who Dwelt in the Temple raised their voices together in the Canticle of the Shepherd; the acolyte, the Handmaidens, the Guardians, the priest. The Shepherd himself had no part in it but to stand before the people and hear his office celebrated in song.

Hanno stood before the people and thought of all the other Shepherds who had stood there before him, especially of those who had lived and died in less enlightened times.

Once he would have waited here knowing that afterwards they were going to stick a knife in his throat. Can it really be done by one man, or did they fall on him as they fell on me last night? If the sacrifice truly despaired one man could do it. No wonder the Shepherd was chosen by lot. No wonder he was unwilling, poor bastard.

They think I have despaired. They think I will consent. They think I will consent to say what they want me to say.

I will not.

What will I say?

The singing ended. The piper throttled his instrument and the music died. The priest took Hanno by the arm and drew him forward until he stood between the posts of the sanctuary gate.

'Listen, people,' cried the priest. 'Listen to the witness of the Ritual Shepherd to whom was given the honour of finding the Prophet Dead, with No Mark on him.'

There was a great shout from the well of the temple. Ah, god, thought Hanno. How nasty your people are.

'Hear him!'

Also, god, let me get through this without fainting, because if I do I shall certainly fall down the steps and break my neck. Don't let my nose bleed, don't let me throw up; just let me be Hanno again until I finish. After that we'll have to take our chances, won't we? He stepped forward.

'I am the Shepherd, Chosen by the god, who Stands before the god and Calls upon him in the name of the people.

'I am the Shepherd of whom it was said, He shall bleed in the face. He shall fear death by water. He shall fear the dark. He shall be the most unwilling Shepherd that the Temple has ever known.' Also, I am losing my sight, but no one speaks of this. Who would believe a witness who was half-blind?

'These are the Words of the Prophet who knew me before I came.

'And the Prophet said to the Shepherd, When the Day of the Serpent Cometh, the sky shall open like the mouth of the Basilisk, and my Head shall be cloven like a cheese, and my Spirit shall be Taken Up and the cleft shall close and there shall be No Mark on me.

'The Day of the Serpent has Come, and the Prophet has been Taken Up, and there was No Mark on him. The Shepherd has seen this thing and knows that it is true.'

All the time he was speaking, his words were punctuated with jubilant shouts of 'Shepherd! Shepherd!' and when he paused the entire assembly took up the cry.

If only they would call me by name, I would know what to say. Aram said, You have no name. You are the Shepherd. Dow told me, When you put on that head-dress you are the Ritual Shepherd. You are no longer Hanno. The people do not see you, they see the Shepherd.

True. True. But if they could see me they'd remember who I was. Hanno the boatman, a sore trial to his father, but nice enough for all that.

I was liked once.

Are you out there Father? Ivo? What shall I say? Anise, remember me.

The shouts died away. The priest had stilled them with an uplifted hand.

'All who have gathered here,' he said, 'listen to the Shepherd tell of the Miracle.'

That means you too, said Hanno to the god. So listen.

He began his dialogue.

'It was told me by the Prophet that I should find him Dead with No Mark on him. And so did I find him.'

'And where did you find him?'

'I found him by the Altar where he Dwelt, serving the god, living in the Most Holy Place.' Where I was meant to find him.

'And what did he hold in his Hand?'

'In his one Hand he did hold the Vessel of the Sacrifice and in the other he did hold the Remnant of the god's Garment.' They drove me before them.

'And you looked upon him?'

'And I looked upon him.' I fell over him. Over *him*, Cariola.

'And he Fell in your sight?'

'And he Fell in my sight.' He did not fall in my sight because he was already dead. I thought I might have done it, which was ridiculous, but Dow knew I hadn't. He knew because he had killed him himself.

'He was then Dead?'

'He was then Dead.' Dow killed him because he was more use dead than alive.

'With No Mark on him?'

'With No Mark on him.' And I know now how it was done but I can't prove it. Who would believe me?

What shall I say?

'His Head was Cloven open and he was Taken Up by the hand of the god, and there was No Mark on him,' said the priest.

'The god had nothing to do with it,' said Hanno. He raised his hands and lifted the head-dress. A great sigh of surprise swept round the well of the temple as the Shepherd vanished, and in his place stood a bedraggled young man with a long, pale face and nervous eyes that squinted vaguely past the flattened curve of his nose. 'There is no Shepherd. There is no Prophet. There is no Miracle. He didn't die by the hand of the god. I killed him.'

The sigh was suddenly drawn in again, in one astounded gasp. Hanno was very conscious of Dow's enraged and incredulous face, a few feet away. How long have I got before he decides what to do? That may be a ritual spear he's holding, but it's sharp. Egil too.

'There is a kind of killing that leaves no mark, and I know it.' They would have had to hold me down but Aram never knew what was coming. 'It is the work of a second, and I know it. It is the Secret Knowledge, and I know it.' They thought I was too far gone to understand. 'I murdered a madman. He plagued the life out of me and I killed him. No prophet, no miracle; just a murder. No Shepherd, only me. Hanno. My name is called Hanno.'

Dow moved. Egil moved. Hanno dropped the head-dress and swung his staff in a semicircle before him. Dow sprang back as the horned tip missed him by inches, and Egil, seeing the head-dress roll down the steps towards him, recoiled as though it still contained a head. The amazed mutterings exploded in a shriek of 'Sacrilege!'

Hanno staggered backwards, through the gateway and into the sanctuary, kicking the gate shut behind him; and ran. He did not need to look back to discover that no one was following him. All the Guardians were wearing boots and no one might enter the sanctuary unless barefoot. The priest was spinning, urging, gesticulating. Through the bars of the gate Hanno saw Dow and Egil struggle with thongs and buckles in an effort to remove their footwear. He scrambled over the railing, praying that he would reach the door of the Guardians' hall before it occurred to someone to run round the other way and cut off his escape. He heard feet, saw movement, hurled himself at the open door. Behind him the whole temple was on the move, surging purposelessly; in front of him the hall stretched away towards the sunlight, the yard, the scaffolding. He slammed the first door in the faces of his pursuers. There was no key in the lock and no time to shoot the bolts. He ran down the middle of the long room, seeing nothing but the rectangle of sunshine ahead of him, bisected by the single vertical of the scaffolding. The door from the temple burst open and the Guardians came through like one hunter with a hundred legs, but he was already at the other doorway. He dived through it, into the light, seizing the handle as he went by, and wrenching the door shut behind him. Now for the scaffold, the long climb, and the long dive, and then –

The door had not shut. As it was about to close, a daring hand flashed out and caught him by the sleeve, trying to pull him back. He turned and clung to the handle, an iron hoop as big as a chaplet, summoning all the remains of his will to resist. The sleeve was pulled taut against the edge of the door by the unknown hand, and his own hand was drawn inexorably into the crack. If he or his adversary did not give way in a second, he was going to lose all his fingers. He sank down on the step, swinging on the handle with all his weight, and the door suddenly crashed shut as if someone else's weight had been flung against it. A secret accomplice, come to his aid? Then he heard, unbelievably, the sound of the bolts shot home on the other side, and saw why he had been allowed to win the struggle.

He had shut his own sleeve in the door.

He tried to jerk himself free, but twist and tug as he might, it would not let him go.

Oh, god, is that grateful? he said. The fullness of the sleeve was all trapped on the other side so that the fabric was drawn tight against his forearm, and it was good, expensive fabric, in honour of the Festival, far better quality than anything he normally wore. His own tunic would have ripped like wet paper.

He had to get out of it. The scaffolding was waiting, his ladder to safety, and the sand was running and running. Give me time, give me time; oh god, give me time. With his free hand he began to fumble at the links of his belt, searching for the hinged one that would release it, but it was buried in the fleece of the sheepskin and while he searched he felt a figure come between him and the light. A shadow fell across the door. He looked up, and there were the Guardians.

The yard was small and they filled it, crowding in one behind the other through the narrow arch, until the sun went out and he sat in twilight.

'That was not well done,' said Dow.

'No,' said Hanno. 'I should have remembered the sleeves.'

'That's not entirely what I meant,' said Dow, 'but you're quite right. You look uncommonly silly like that.'

Hanno nodded and reflected that perhaps it was no bad thing for people to believe that a fool had died nobly. Just then he was almost inclined to regret having denied Aram his miraculous departure. There was nothing remotely noble about his own situation. At any moment Dow was going to skewer him to the door, and all he could do about it was sit and wait, with one arm raised above his head as though he were vainly trying to attract someone's attention.

'Does he understand what he's done?' Egil demanded, pushing up alongside Dow. 'Take him back in there and let him see what he's done.'

'Are the people very distressed?' said Hanno. 'I'm sorry. I didn't want to upset them.' I don't care if anyone's upset. What am I talking about?

'Upset? Damn that!' Egil shouted, in his face. 'You

defiled the Vestments. You denied the Ritual. You lied to the people.'

'Well, I couldn't tell them the truth, could I?' said Hanno. 'No one would have believed it.'

The Guardians drew closer, in a mass: the mass bristled with spear-heads.

'The Book is the truth,' said Egil.

'No. The Book is a lie. The Book will say whatever you want it to say, but the truth is that one of you murdered a harmless idiot because his death could be made use of. If I'd said that, I'd have been shouted down as a liar; but I said I did it, and they believe that, don't they? It's not true, but it's nearer the truth than you'll ever get. Aram was nothing, and he's still nothing.'

'He's a holy Prophet!' Egil shrieked. Hanno shrank back against the door. He means it. He believes it himself.

Dow put a restraining hand on Egil's shoulder.

'Shepherd,' he said, 'why did you do it?'

'If I'd refused to testify you would have kept me here for ever. You would never have let me stand before the people.'

'What is he saying?' The question came from beyond the Guardians, and the mass parted – cloven like a cheese – and the priest came through. 'What has he told you?'

'He says that if he had refused to testify we would have kept him here for ever,' said Egil.

'Or killed me.'

'No.'

'You're going to kill me now,' said Hanno. He had been fully aware of this from the moment that the door closed on his sleeve, but the sound of his own voice declaring it suddenly presented the idea as an imminent fact. Somehow, they would have their revenge, and how better than to carry out last night's threat?

'No,' said the priest again. 'No one is going to kill you.'

'They killed Aram.'

'No, no, no.'

'No,' said Dow.

The priest was actually smiling. 'No, no, no, no.'

It was the smile that finished him off. He crouched as close to the door as he could and curled up, like an endangered woodlouse.

'No. No.'

'No.'

'No, no, no.'

'Human sacrifice. First Aram; now me.'

'It must be your extreme youth that makes you speak so eagerly of dying,' said the priest. 'Old men do not wish to die.'

'Nor did Aram,' said Hanno. 'Nor do I.'

'If you thought Aram didn't want to die,' said the priest, 'why did you kill him?'

'I didn't kill him.'

'But you did. We all heard you tell the people that you killed him.'

'You know I didn't,' Hanno cried.

'Then why did you say that you did?' said Dow.

'I told you –'

'Then tell me,' said the priest.

'The people had to be told – there was no miracle.' Hanno felt himself begin to shake, and braced his back against the door. 'There was no miracle. I thought that if I was kept here, or killed, no one would ever know what had happened. At least now they know there was no miracle.'

'There was a miracle,' said the priest. 'As you will see.'

'No miracle,' said Hanno. 'A sacrifice – no miracle. No miracle.'

'He's been looking at the old tapestry,' said Dow. 'It should have been destroyed.'

'Last night you said I could die like a sheep, unheard,

unseen. You took me by the hair and held a knife to my throat.'

More smiling.

'No.'

'No, no, no.'

'No, no, no, no.'

'*You did*,' he shouted hopelessly, at their blank, rational faces.

'Who did?' said Egil. 'I don't understand you. Who did what?'

'But you were there,' said Hanno, assailed by a fearful doubt.

'Where was I?'

'Last night in the temple – in the dark – you were waiting for me; you caught me and held me and Dow – and Dow –'

'You seem to have had a wonderful dream, my son,' said the priest.

Hanno looked up at the taut sleeve and at his hand, drooping helplessly from the wrist. The fingers closed over the palm and made a fist: a peninsular act of defiance that had nothing to do with the despair at the other end of his arm. 'It was no dream.'

'Tell me what happened,' said the priest. 'But do not add to your sufferings by obstinacy. I think you may discover that you are mistaken.'

'It was no dream. When the bell rang I went to the door of the hall of the Guardians, and I knocked; and when it was opened I asked for a companion in my vigil.'

'That's true,' said Arlo. 'I was Keeper of the Door last night. It happened as he says.'

'I asked for the fellow whose eyebrows meet in the middle. I couldn't remember his name.'

'That's also correct,' said Arlo. 'And I delivered the message.'

'He delivered it to me,' said a voice at the back. A sturdy youth with a hairy face pushed his way to the front. Hanno looked at him with dislike.

'I still can't remember your name.'

The youth, whose eyebrows met head-on over his nose, like amorous caterpillars, returned the look.

'Straightway I took my spear and went to the Hut of the Shepherd. The Shepherd was lying on the floor of the Hut, asleep, as though he had fallen asleep at his prayers.'

'It wasn't the first time it happened,' said another voice.

'But not last night,' said Hanno. He saw where they were all headed. Lies grew best close to the truth.

'What did happen, then?' asked the priest.

'I waited for a long time, but no one came. So I went across the sanctuary, to the colonnade.'

'You should not have left your Vigil, my son,' said the priest, and lifted a humorous eyebrow. 'Even in a dream.'

'And when I went back to the hut, they were waiting for me, in the dark. Dow and Egil I saw –'

'In the dark?' said Dow.

'You had a lantern.'

'Ah.'

'But there were others. Six at least.'

'And what did these six do?' said the priest.

'They know what they did,' said Hanno. 'They dragged me to the ground and held me there, while Dow took out a knife and said I might die like a sheep. But, he said, there were other ways. Then I knew. . .how. . .Aram. . .'

'Why didn't you call for help?' said Egil. 'If six ruffians had jumped on me in the dark I wouldn't have kept quiet about it.'

'You know why I didn't,' said Hanno. He touched his hand to his swollen lip.

'You did that yesterday,' said Dow. 'When I took you to your room. You tripped in the doorway.'

'Tripped!'

'And then what happened?' said the priest.

'Then they left me. And I went back to my hut. And after a while Dow came in to share my vigil,' he said. 'After that, I slept.'

'You slept the whole while,' said the priest. 'You never left the Hut. Rohan here –' he indicated the youth with the single eyebrow – 'will testify to that.'

'You never left the Hut,' said Rohan, activated by a nudge from Egil.

'And by and by,' said the priest, 'I came, as is the custom, to encourage the Shepherd in that his last night as Shepherd. And I found the Shepherd sleeping.'

'And being Friends of the Shepherd, we too came to support him in his Vigil; and we too found him sleeping,' said Egil and Dow and Frey. Hanno heard their voices proceed gravely into the rhythm of a chant.

This is rehearsed. This has been written down. This has become part of the Book.

'The Shepherd slept like a child,' said Dow. 'And we forbore to wake him.'

'It was an Affront to the god,' said Egil. 'But the god will forgive it.'

'The Prophet will intercede for him,' said Frey.

'But you said I fell asleep on the floor,' said Hanno. 'I woke up on the couch. The acolyte saw me. You did that.' He pointed to Dow.

'How clever of you to guess,' said Dow.

'Guessing? I remember.'

'You never woke,' said Dow. 'Not once, all night. You've no need to feel ashamed, Shepherd. It was wrong, but not really your fault. You're very weak – and confused,' he added, meaningly.

'Soon you will be able to sleep for as long as you like,' said the priest.

Sleep? If murder were a miracle, what might sleep be? The secret killer prospered and grew sleek in his prosperity. What was the fate of the confessed murderer, be he never so innocent?

Dow held out his spear, butt foremost, and rapped with it upon the door. Immediately there came an answering tattoo and Hanno, head reverberating with the thuds, felt the bolts drawn back behind him. The great hoop of the handle turned and the door opened far enough to release the trapped sleeve, before closing again. His arm fell free.

'Come,' said the priest, making uplifting gestures with his cupped hands.

'On your feet, Shepherd,' said Egil.

'Where are we going?'

'Not very far.'

'I thought I should die here,' said Hanno, half to himself. He pressed his hands against the door, and levered himself upright, out of the pit of shadows at the feet of the Guardians; and beyond them, in the little yard, the sun still shone. Among them stood the weighty leg of the scaffolding. Now that he had time to observe it closely he saw that it was a single pine trunk, stripped of bark, as smooth as his staff. There was not a foothold on it.

'The Shepherd is not going to die,' said the priest.

'Am I still Shepherd?'

'Until you leave us you are still Shepherd.'

'And then I shall die?'

'You will not die by our hands,' said the priest. 'The dying is all done.'

'I don't believe you,' said Hanno.

'You may believe or not, as you please. It makes no difference now,' said Egil. Hanno looked at the spear in Egil's hand, and the knife in Dow's belt.

Dow and the priest came close and turned him to face the door, taking him each by the hand. Hanno thought he had been mauled and manhandled enough, and he tried to withdraw his hands, but could not. Dow's short fingers were hard and firm with the Knowledge that Makes a Small Man Great, and wrestling with the priest would be like pitting himself against a baby. He could free himself from that ancient lock, but only with unforgivable violence, and the old man knew it. He had always known it: they had all of them always known it, and Hanno had known it too, from the moment he sealed his fate with that first submission, when he had allowed the priest to shake him breathless. Now he longed to hear the powdery crunch of old bones, but when he tried to clench his hand over the priest's knuckles he knew that he had left it too late.

Egil came round from behind and surveyed the three of them doubtfully.

'Do you think he can walk so far?'

'The god will keep him on his feet for as long as is needful,' said the priest.

I hope you heard that, god. I am to die standing up. See to it.

Egil's eyes were still on him, still full of mistrust.

'Should we gag him?'

No.

'No, no. He has nothing to say now.'

Egil stepped up and threw open the door. Dow and the priest walked forward, through the doorway that was wide enough to admit three men walking abreast, and between them went the Shepherd, into the hall of the Guardians. Now he had plenty of time to look about him as they proceeded down the barrack at a measured pace, but again he saw nothing, only the approaching door which, as they came up to it, was opened from the other side. Supported by the Guardian and the priest, and by his own stubborn refusal to fall, the Shepherd entered the temple for the last time.

The temple was silent with the silence of ten thousand breathing people. The musicians stood upon the steps, the Handmaidens flanked the altars, the Guardians spread out round the colonnade with upraised spears. Hanno, so far as he thought anything, thought they would go round the railing and come out at the head of the steps, but they went the other way, towards the Cell of the Prophet, and approached the altar from behind.

Not here, oh god, not here. Not at the altar with the fingers in the hair and the knife at the throat. We are enlightened now. We do not kill a man in the sight of the people. We kill him in the dark and call it a miracle. Rose, lily, sorrel, hemlock, clover, lily, rose. . .

No, not the altar. . .

The steps? Aconite, sorrel, mallow, arum, windflower, spurge, rose, lily. . .

Dow and the priest led him on to the gate of the sanctuary and stopped at the top of the steps.

Here?

He looked at the faces below him and knew that he would not die here. From all those mouths issued a vague sigh of disappointment as the people realized that they would not see the Shepherd suffer death for what he had done. Dow had been wrong to think that the sacrifice had been abandoned because the people did not like it. The people would have liked it very much indeed.

Dow and the priest raised their arms and Hanno's arms were raised too, as if in triumph.

'Behold!' the priest cried. 'Behold the Instrument of the god. Behold the Shepherd who was made the Instrument of the god that the words of the Prophet might be fulfilled.'

Egil and Frey joined them on the steps.

'When the Day of the Serpent was Come, the Prophet sat in the Most Holy Place, and the god did see him, and the god called to his Prophet. And the Prophet said to the god, How shall I go? And the god put a great Anger into the Heart of his Shepherd, and by the Hand of the Shepherd was the Prophet slain, that his words might be fulfilled, and he was Taken Up, and there was No Mark on him. The Shepherd stands before you, the Instrument of the god, and his Name shall be written into the Book that he shall be known to all who come after. And when the Prophet is worshipped, so shall he be worshipped.'

Not my name. Sweet god, not my name.

Hanno stood transfixed and felt the worship beginning. A strange sound surged about his feet, and swelled, and billowed. They were calling to him, 'Hanno, Haanno, Haaaanno, Haaaaanno': ten thousand breathing sheep.

'Go!' shouted the priest, hideously rejuvenated, above the bleating. 'Go to your homes and make ready to honour the Turning of the Year. Tomorrow shall see a new season and a new Shepherd. Go.'

The gate opened and the people went towards it. Hanno saw a murky river swirling across the courtyard and boiling through the gateway, and still they held him there, arms lifted as if in triumph, until the last of the ten thousand had gone and the temple was empty of all but those who Dwelt in it. And the Shepherd.

His hands were released. Egil turned to him and unfastened the bronze belt. He stepped back and made room for Frey who pulled away the sheepskin. Hanno, who had sweated and cursed beneath its weight, shivered as it was taken from him.

'You may go now,' said the priest. 'You are no longer the Shepherd. You may go. You must go.'

He was pushed, gently, towards the colonnade, and as he reached it the colonnade drew back in disdain and left him alone in the courtyard. Before him was the open gate; behind him. . .behind him?

He turned and looked. The Dwellers in the Temple had

gone also. There were no Guardians in the colonnade, no Handmaidens on the steps, no musicians, no acolyte, no priest at altar. Only, in the shadows, he could see the red eye of the sanctuary lamp, watching him go.

He took three steps more and turned again, but this time even the eye was closed to him. There was only the open gate now. He closed his own eyes and fell, unconscious before he hit the pavement.

16

HE wakes in darkness with a single red star above him, and thinks at first that he lies on the altar, bound and stricken and dying. But he feels flints under his head; one inquiring hand discovers pebbles and moss, the other locates a wooden wall, with studs as large as a fist. He is stretched out at the foot of the gate, no longer in the courtyard but on the other side, in the narrow lane that leads to the city. In the unclear distance he sees the open canyon of steep walls and as he watches, the soft enormous moon floats like a flower between them.

He has left the temple. Those that Dwell in the Temple have honoured their promise and let him go, but when he comes to think how they let him go he sits sadly by the gate, knowing that they found him in his faint, dragged him out of their precinct and closed the gate upon him, leaving him to recover or not. This is no more than he expected, after all, but he is now back in the city, in his own world; he must have lain there for hours, and no one has come near him.

He raises himself from the ground, very stiff but unhurt by his fall, and rests for a while on the mounting block where he sat last year, to watch the family of the retiring Shepherd wait eagerly for their son to be returned to them. There is no one waiting for *him*. He thinks how he has sustained himself during the past year with anticipation of the moment when he leaves the temple and walks – no, surely, runs – to the gate where his father and Ivo stand to greet him.

They are not there. They never have been there. He remains on the mounting block, embracing his own shoulders, and considers this for a long time. The Shepherd has not been greeted when he leaves the temple because the Shepherd has not left the temple. He is there for ever, impaled on the ritual, and the poor creature who has been thrown out to lie in the dark at the foot of the gate is nothing but a discarded husk. The Ritual Murderer will be worshipped in the temple, but outside the temple there is no ritual, only a murderer.

Who will take flowers from a killer's hands?

He detaches himself from the mounting block and walks slowly to the end of the lane.

You didn't kill anyone, he reminds himself.

Who will believe that, after what you did?

He has reached the end of the lane and wanders out into the deserted streets of the city, where he last walked with the Guardian after his flight and recapture in Potter's Street. Now he may go where he likes, and no one will bring him back. Overhead the lime trees are in flower, but the scent is overpowered by a charred odour that comes from somewhere else, carried on the night wind.

He follows it, for want of anything else to follow, down streets and alleys, until he comes to the market place; and here he finally discovers (when he no longer cares) what he missed during those years when he stayed at home and celebrated the Festival with his family. All the stalls have been felled and removed and, in the centre of the square, fires have been lit. Over each fire the carcase of a sheep turns on a spit. Round each fire dance the people, the same people who cried out to him this morning, because he slew the Prophet: somewhere among them the next Shepherd.

As he watches, the dancers about one fire break the ring and make their way, in line, towards the next. As they pass it the dancers there break their ring and follow the others;

and so at every fire until nothing remains but an undulating serpent that writhes in and out of the flames, shouting wordlessly all along its length. It appears, to him, to be enjoying itself. He would walk across the square to reach the alley that leads to the river, because it is the nearest way and the fires are bright.

But he knows that he cannot walk across the path of the serpent, neither tonight, nor any other night, nor by day. The serpent might trample him down in its witless excitement, but what will men do when they meet him and know him? He walks round the square in the shadows; when the serpent dances too close he shrinks into a doorway or the mouth of a passage, and in one of these he comes upon three children, playing a game. One child kneels on the ground, holding in his small hands a rag of linen and a potsherd; another stands behind him, who with stiff fingers makes mystical signs about the head of the first. The kneeling child collapses in a heap and the standing child darts away to fetch a third, who stands apart; shocked hands held up like squirrel's paws. The second child comes back, and points at the fallen one. 'There is no mark on him.'

He walks on, cleaving to the walls, until he reaches the alley that leads to the river. Last time he walked here the Guardian walked behind him. Here is the place where he sat and refused to move, and here is the water, a long way down and black. Here is the bridge and here the steps where he turned and threatened to kick his Friend into the river. And here is the grass and the garden; here is his home.

The house is watchful, white outside and dark within. All around him it is dark, and by his side is the river; no shallow fountain or narrow bath house, but a deep and moving stream that can drown a man and has drowned many. He is no longer afraid of the water, or the darkness. His head aches brutally, but his nose does not bleed. All that is the matter of the Ritual Shepherd, and the Ritual Shepherd is still in the temple. He sits in the dark, by the river, and rests his aching head on the cold grass. He waits. Once when he looks up he thinks he sees a lamp flutter behind a window, and an anxious shadow blinks across a blind, but no one comes out to him, and he realizes that the people inside are waiting too. He rises and walks to the fence, where he stands and remains standing until he can be certain that someone has seen him. An empty house is an *empty* house, and this house is not empty. He senses life inside it, but no one comes out to him.

Once he knows that however long he stands there no one will ever come out to him again, he turns and walks beside the river until he comes to the bridge and the long-desired elder tree. The white dishes of the elder-flowers glow a little in the night and it seems to him that by their light alone he sces his boat moored as he left it, beneath the branches of the tree.

Supporting his weight on the trunk he treads down the bank and steps into the boat. It rocks like a cradle to receive him and he would like to lie down in it and let the water lull him a little, but he casts off and lets the current draw the boat out into the middle of the river, before turning its bow upstream. The river is running high after the rain and he has to row strongly, surprised that in his condition he can still row at all. As he passes below the wall of the temple the moon casts a shadow like a net across the water, but he does not see it. The net already contains all it needs.

That was Ram's Bridge; now Cart Bridge and Horse Ferry; after the bridges the meadows, and then the villages, Goat Lees and Cow Lees, Alder Fen, Thorn Eye and Ram's Eye. Here are the meadows, but he will never reach the villages, not even the first village. He was mistaken. He cannot row. His whole chest is a burning harness and his breath sticks like a knife in his throat.

So when the river turns he does not turn with it, but

brings the boat to rest among rushes, at a place where the low bank is pocked with rabbit holes. He ships the oars and eases himself over the side, reeling knee-deep in water and weeds until he stumbles against the dry land and there lies down.

The boat slides silently away.

All night he lies there; the dew falls on him as he watches the wheel of the sky arch over his head. It is a white wheel, traced in milk, very indistinct to his eyes. It does not turn. The earth turns, as any fool must know. He can feel it turn, but who will believe him? Fires glow on the skyline, but he prefers not to look at them; only when the whole eastern sky turns to rose does he lower his eyes to watch the sun come up. It is the first sunrise he has seen for a year, and out of it ride three travellers with foreign voices.

They look down at him from their high horses, evidently dismayed by his appearance. They assume that he has fallen among thieves, since he is clearly sick and destitute; an assumption which is confirmed when they ask him what has happened.

'Are you hurt?'

He nods.

'Have you lost everything?'

Again, he nods.

'Where do you come from?'

'What is your name?'

'What is your name?'

'What is your name?'

He stares at them, quite speechless.